LESSONS

FROM LIFE

FOR LIFE

from the New Testament

Wesley L. Gerig, PhD.

published by
Fort Wayne Alumni and Friends Resource Center

915 W. Rudisill Blvd.
Fort Wayne, IN 46807
260.744.8790
email: alumnifw@taylor.edu
web: http://fw.taylor.edu/store

Introduction

God's guidance for a divinely-approved life comes from His Word, in three major ways. Many passages, and especially the ethical sections of the New Testament books, contain directly-stated PRESCRIPTIONS. For examples, note the following: "Stop owing anything to anyone but continue loving one another" (Romans 13:8); "Stop being overcome by evil (done to you), but continue overcoming evil with goodness" (Romans 12:21); "Don't give the holy thing to the dogs nor throw your pearls before the swine" (Matthew 7:6); and "Continue rejoicing in the Lord always; and again I will say (it), continue rejoicing." (Philippians 4:4)

A second way we receive guidance for living is via the general PRINCIPLES found in various sections of the Bible. One clear principle is that we are to do all we do for God's glory, not man's. (I Corinthians 10:31). Another principle stressed in two major sections of the New Testament is that we are not to hurt a weaker brother (or sister) in Christ (Romans 14:1-15:5 and I Corinthians 8:1-11:1). As another principle one might cite the directive to protect our bodies, which are not our own, as Christians, and are actually sanctuaries of the Holy Spirit who lives in them. (I Corinthians 6:19, 20) A fourth one is in a verse that emphasizes the need for full assurance of the rightness of any action before we do it, Romans 14:23b: "Whatever we cannot do with the firm conviction it is right is sin or wrong for us."

The third means of guidance may be the most difficult means of gaining instruction and that is from PICTURES portrayed by the lives of the Old and New Testament characters. Many lessons from the lives of these people can be learned for life today as we study the events that happened to them. As the Apostle Paul said twice in I Corinthians 10, the things which happened to the biblical figures occurred as examples for us, and they were written down for our instruction. (See I Corinthians 10:6, 11) Consequently, the narratives in our Old and New Testaments were not just written down for our INFORMATION but for our EDIFICATION to help us avoid today the pitfalls which certain biblical figures experienced and achieve today the victories which some of them enjoyed.

The purpose of this book is to help pastors, Sunday school teachers, youth leaders, parents, and even individual Christians develop an ability to draw out lessons from the narratives in the Bible. As a result, our teaching of the Bible should not only be factually accurate but also practically and ethically beneficial. With this technique to make the Bible stories relevant to current Christian living, no one should be able to say of a lesson taught or a sermon heard, "That was so much interesting information, but so what? How should this affect my living today?" The lessons from biblical lives should then become immediately and clearly apparent for current Christian living.

How to use this book...

The best and most helpful biblical study is one that is balanced with adequate time spent on gaining a knowledge of the facts of a biblical event and also some time given to drawing practical lessons from that event for current living. This present volume was prepared particularly to help Christian leaders (pastors, Sunday school teachers, and leaders of small groups) to see possible ways to teach and apply Old Testament events for their people.

The various lists of lessons which I have set forth in this book are in no way exhaustive lists; and any group of thinking Christians should be able to come up with other practical applications from the individual biblical events discussed here, if given time to think. In fact, their suggestions may be better than mine and even more relevant to each group and individual members of the group than the ones I have cited. By all means, when possible, give your group members opportunities to think of their own applications and do not stifle their thought processes by giving them any from my lists until they have had opportunities to think for themselves.

There are four dangers which a leader of any group studying New Testament history and using the material in this volume as a guide must avoid.

1. INCOMPLETENESS
One is incompleteness of his or her study of any biblical text before trying to lead a discussion centered on that biblical material. Be sure to use biblical commentaries, Bible dictionaries and other materials related to the New Testament story under discussion. Know your material thoroughly, especially if it includes verses whose meanings are difficult to ascertain. Give attention to persons, places and things of importance. Use maps to locate geographical places mentioned in the biblical text and to discover distances between places which are often important for an understanding of the text. Identify the people who play an important part in the narrative.

To aid you in your discovery of the facts related to any given biblical passage, answer the interrogative words which someone has called "my six honest serving men, who taught me all I knew, namely, what and where, and how, and when, and why and who!" Answer these questions in your own personal study of the biblical text first and then later use them with your groups:

  A. What are the things which appear in the text?
  B. Where do the events or the event occur?
  C. How were results in the text achieved?
  D. When did the events happen?
  E. Why did certain things take place?
  F. And who were the people involved in the action?

Be sure you can correctly pronounce all difficult names of people and places and can pronounce and define any difficult words which appear in the biblical passage under review.

2. IMBALANCE

A second danger to avoid, as a responsible leader of discussion is IMBALANCE. Some leaders tend to slight the biblical text and hasten on to what they consider possibly the more helpful and perhaps the more interesting discussion, namely the application of the text to current life's circumstances. Some who allow insuffcient time for teaching and preaching spend too much time on explaining the text and, because they have run out of time for application, justify their omission by saying to themselves and some even aloud to their group, "You apply the teaching for yourselves." Plan your teaching and preaching time so that you have adequate time to explain carefully your biblical text so that your congregation or class members leave with a better understanding of a portion of Scripture. Then, using your own thoughts, those observations of your hearers and my volume to apply the biblical truth, relate the biblical text to current Christian living.

In the process, your congregation or class should learn how to make the historical sections of the Bible much more practical and meaningful for themselves.

3. INCLUSION

A third peril for a leader of a group study is the INCLUSION in one presentation of all the lessons found in this book for a given passage. Why not zero in on two or three applications of the text gained from your own study or from this volume and save some others for a sermon or Bible study on the same biblical passage. To try to cover too much material at one time, whether factual or applicatory or both, can be overwhelming for the hearers and can result in very little being remembered or put into practice.

4. IGNORING

A final danger can be the IGNORING of any contributions to the study by the group members. Some of the most important and memorable applications of a biblical event my not be those found in this book but may well be those which are suggested by the group. Allow your hearers time to think up their own lessons and add those that are different than mine to my list.

With these warnings in mind, my hope is that you will do all you can to develop an ability to make your teaching from the New Testament as practical and profitable as possible. Then also strive to help your hearers learn to master the ability of applying for their own situations today what happened to the people in the New Testament. After all, the Apostle Paul wrote, "Now these things happened to them as an example [for us]; and they were written for our instruction upon whom the ends of the ages have come" [I Corinthians 10:6, 11]. Since this is inspired truth, we must learn by our own perception and practice how to uncover for ourselves practical helps for holy living from the New Testament happenings and then seek to pass on the ability to do this to those who sit under our ministry. May our God help us to succeed in this important and very worthwhile endeavor.

Dr. Wes Gerig
October, 2012

Table of Contents

Luke 60

12

Matthew

NEEDS A PERSON MAY HAVE-Matthew 6:5-14

Lessons about NEEDS A PERSON MAY HAVE from Jesus' teaching about praying

1. Needs a person may have are both temporal and spiritual and both kinds can and should be prayed for. (e.g. God's kingdom or reign and our bread)
2. They all are of interest to our heavenly Father.
3. They should be prayed for as specifically as the pray-er can do it.
4. They can be requests for the provision of some kinds of needs or deliverance from other kinds.
5. They may include a need to obtain forgiveness for some sins committed.
6. They will be taken care of as we trust God for His help in whatever way He chooses to give it.
7. They are known by one's heavenly Father before they are prayed for, but this should not be a reason for not asking for His help.
8. They should not be a cause for worry but for prayer and waiting for the Father's answer.
9. They may not be "needs" as the Father sees them from His vantage point and consequently they may not be answered or at least not answered immediately. (See also Philippians 4:19 where Paul declares that his God will supply all our "needs," but not all our "wants.")
10. They may seem little or even foolish to the person in need but this should not be an excuse for not spreading them out before the Lord in prayer. (As someone has said, "If a need is too small to be made into a prayer, it is too small to be made into a burden.")

PRAYING-Matthew 6:5-14

Lessons about PRAYING from Jesus' teaching about prayer

1. Praying does not have to be long to be heard.
2. It is an important characteristic and constant exercise of a true disciple of the Lord.
3. It should be as specific as the need for which we are praying.

4. It is a necessary exercise if we are to get our needs cared for by our heavenly Father. (See James 4:2b)
5. It is effective only if done by people who are holding no grudges against others. (See especially Matthew 5:14-15 and also Psalms 66:18)
6. It should not be entered into for the purpose of receiving the praise of others around us.
7. It is often a cry for help from a person who needs it.
8. It is an indication that the pray-ers trust their heavenly Father for His help with their problems.
9. It must be directed to the correct source of help, our Father.
10. It is simply conversational communication with God, our Father.
11. It should include, either explicitly or certainly implicitly, that God's will be done.
12. It can include supplication for all kinds of needs, spiritual and/or material.
13. It can be exercised for communal needs. (e.g. "our daily bread," "our debts," etc.)
14. It is a practice that indicates the pray-er's faith in God for His help.
15. It can include worship and praise to God for who He is, not just requests with which we need His help. (e.g. "Let your name be hallowed.")
16. It is not the pray-er's prescribing for God but only pleading with God to help us in whatever way He sees fit.
17. It should be exercised with a proper attitude on the part of the pray-er, namely, that God's will be done.
18. It should involve the pray-er's undivided attention and concentration. (Note Matthew 6:6 and references to "the inner room" and "the closing of the door")
19. It should be a day-to-day practice for needs for each individual day.
20. It can gain for the pray-er God's help so that he or she is not fighting the battles against testing and temptation alone.

PRAYER-Matthew 14:22-33

Lessons about PRAYER from Peter's prayer for help as he began to sink in the Sea of Galilee (See particularly Matthew 14:30 "Lord, save me.")

1. Prayer should be the first recourse when faced with any problem, especially the life-threatening kind.
   It does not necessarily demand a great deal of faith to succeed. (See the Lord's words to Peter in v. 31 "O you of little faith, why did you doubt?")
2. It in itself is an indicator of some faith in the Lord and His ability to help.
3. It does not have to be long to be heard.
4. It is the only recourse for help for many of our needs.
5. It must be directed to the only One who can do something about the need.
6. It can be made at any time in any situation.
7. It can be made for personal needs.
8. It can change our circumstances, not just ourselves in relation to our circumstances.
9. It may be offered by a person already in the middle of a great crisis in life, even one of his or her own making. (Peter took his eyes off the Lord and got his eyes on the lake and the storm and he began to sink.)
10. It must be exercised to be effective. (See James 4:2b)
11. It can grow out of the experience of a physical need.
12. It may be our only hope in seemingly hopeless situations in life.
13. It is the God-ordained way to tap into God's unlimited divine power.
    It does not demand a certain location for prayer, a certain posture in prayer, or a certain jargon for prayer to be heard. ("Help, Lord!" is enough.)

MARRIAGE-Matthew 19:3-12

Lessons about MARRIAGE which can be learned from Jesus' remarks

1. Marriage is a bond between two people, a male and a female, that is intended by God to be permanent and complementary.

2. It is a very serious relationship and for that reason Jesus implies that it should not be entered into except after very serious thought, good counsel, and earnest prayer.
3. It is the closest relationship existing on the human level, closer even than the one existing between parent and child. vv. 56 "one flesh"
4. It is never intended to end in divorce but is intended to continue until death breaks the bond.

   Appendix: It was intended at the beginning of time to correct the one thing that God said was not good in His creation, namely, that man should be alone. (See Genesis 2:18-25)

DIVORCE-Matthew 19:3-12

Lessons about DIVORCE which can be learned from Jesus' teaching

1. Divorce was never intended by God when He instituted marriage.
2. It will never take place if the two marriage partners will live according to God's Word.
3. It is a dangerous practice that sets the partners legally free to commit immorality.
4. It is discussed here with an exceptive phrase involving the Greek word "porneia," which is very hard to interpret.
5. It humanly and legally separates a bond that is the closest there is on the human level. ("one flesh")
6. It violates a command of God which warns against mans separating what God has joined together. v. 6
7. It is an ancient but hateful and hurtful practice.
8. It should be avoided at all legitimate costs.
9. It is something that should only transpire in the most severe marital situations.
10. It may be permitted in order to prevent the cruelty of vicious husbands toward their wives and vice versa.
11. It should never be entered into ignorantly, quickly, or ill advisedly.
12. It indicates an unwillingness on the part of one or both of the marriage partners to forgive.

18

13. It can happen when one is ignorant of what God's Word teaches or knows what it teaches but is unwilling to obey it.
14. It involves the breaking of a solemn vow made before God and often many witnesses.
15. It generally happens because one partner or both partners want their ways, not God's way.

THE LORD'S RETURN-Matthew 24

Lessons about THE LORD'S RETURN

1. The Lord's return will happen when many people will not expect it.
2. It should be an encouragement for Christians to live rightly and fulfill all their responsibilities faithfully.
3. It will result in rewards or punishments, depending on how people have lived.
4. It will come suddenly and unexpectedly, especially for unbelievers. (See I Thessalonians 5:26)
5. It will catch some people unawares.
6. It will be on a day and at an hour unknown by any of us.
7. It will bring separation with blessing or cursing.
8. It will involve greater responsibilities in the future as a reward for faithful service now.
9. It should be an encouragement to be found DOING when the Lord returns. (Belief always affects behavior.
10. It is important for each of us to keep it in mind, especially those of us in places of leadership.
11. It should find us DOING the Lord's will as revealed to us in His Word.
12. It is not something that we should worry about as to date.
13. It should not catch believers unprepared.
14. It will be preceded by signs by which the alert Bible student can know that its coming is near.
15. It will be preceded by a severe period of tribulation and terrible convulsions in the heavens.

SERVING THE LORD-Matthew 24:42-51

Lessons about SERVING THE LORD from the experience of the bond-servants

1. Serving the Lord needs to be done consistently well.
2. It receives great rewards if carried out faithfully.
3. It can reap severe consequences if it is done unfaithfully and poorly.
4. It is not to be carried out self-centeredly without regard for one's fellow servants.
5. It can be brought to an end suddenly and unexpectedly.
6. It is to be carried out with a view to the Lord's return and His evaluation of one's service.
7. It will be rewarded with more and greater responsibilities if one's work is evaluated as having been done well and faithfully.
8. It involves doing faithfully what has been assigned to the Lord's bond servants.
9. It should not be characterized by laziness, idleness, or selfish indulgence in luxurious living.
10. It is more easily carried out with good and faithful friends around us and encouraging us, not "drunkards." v. 49

PREPAREDNESS FOR THE LORD'S RETURN-Matthew 25:1-13

Lessons regarding PREPAREDNESS FOR THE LORD'S RETURN as given in the parable of the virgin in Matthew 25:1-13

1. Preparedness for the Lord's return demands careful forethought and constant effort.
2. It will characterize some persons when the Lord returns.
3. It is a "must" if we are to attend the marriage supper with the Bridegroom. (See Revelation 19:7-8 "the righteous acts of the saints")
4. It can be attempted too late to be effective.
5. It demands a diligent and permanent readiness since no one but the Father knows the exact day and hour when the return will occur. (See Matthew 24:36)
6. It demands the personal attention of each true believer.

7. It is something to which we should all give attention while here on this earth.
8. It cannot be done for us by others.
9. It demands more than "just getting by" in the Lord's service.
10. It demands steadfastness in the waiting process.

SERVICE FOR THE LORD-Matthew 25:14-30

Lessons regarding OUR SERVICE FOR THE LORD from the parable of the talents in Matthew 25:14-30

1. Our service for the Lord will have varying success according to the abilities we have been given by the Lord.
2. It is expected by the Lord, whether He says anything about it or not.
3. It is to continue until He returns (or we die first).
4. It will be abundantly rewarded if it has been done faithfully. (See I Corinthians 4:2)
5. It will be punished severely if it is not done faithfully and properly.
6. It will be rewarded at the judgment seat of Christ when He returns (at the Bema). (See II Corinthians 5:10 and Romans 14:10)
7. It may demand long and tiresome effort.
8. It will result in many rewards.
9. It can result in more responsibility if it is carried out faithfully. (e.g. The one talent)
10. It is ongoing until the Lord returns.
11. It should be carried out with wholeheartedness and with gusto.
12. It should be entered into immediately when the responsibility is given.
13. It should be done to the best of our abilities.
14. It should be done without the Lord's eye having to be on us all the time.
15. It will be rewarding for both the Lord and His servants.

WORKING FOR THE LORD-Matthew 25:14-30

Lessons on WORKING FOR THE LORD as given in the parable of the talents in Matthew 25:14-30

1. Working for the Lord will never go unnoticed or unrewarded by the Lord, no matter how insignificant that work may seem to us. (See Matthew 10:42 and "a cup of cold water")
2. It is to be obediently undertaken at once, as soon as the responsibility has been assigned.
3. It is not rewarded according to successfulness as the world looks at it but according to FAITHFULNESS as God sees it. (See I Corinthians 4:2)
4. It demands people of all kinds, some well-endowed with gifts and some less endowed.
5. It should be continued until the Lord returns (or He calls us home to heaven).
6. It is often postponed or neglected altogether by those who seem to be least endowed with talents or think their talent is not important.
7. It may demand that we work alone in isolation from other believers (or cooperatively together, as other passages teach). (See I Corinthians 12)
8. It is expected by the Lord of His bondservants.
9. It will be evaluated at some future judgment time by the Lord.
10. It will result in ultimate joy and satisfaction if carried out faithfully.
11. It requires faith-fullness and faithfulness.
12. It should arise out of a deep and sincere respect and appreciation for the gift or gifts God has entrusted to us.
13. It will result in the faithful workers being rewarded with more gifts and responsibilities in the future.
14. It demands our using of the abilities God has given us.
15. It demands the wise and active use of talents the Lord has loaned to us.

Mark

DEMONS-Mark 1:21-34

Lessons about DEMONS from Jesus' encounter with them recorded in Mark 1:21-34

1. Demons can and do inhabit and possess people.
2. They are real, not imaginary, beings.
3. They know the terrible destiny that is ahead for them.
4. They recognize the power of Jesus and are absolutely subservient to His will.
5. They recognize Jesus of Nazareth, the Holy One of God.
6. They must come out of a person at the command of Jesus.
7. They may use a person's voice to speak.
8. They may exist in quantity in one single individual.
9. They are the same as evil or unclean spirits. (See Mark 1:23)
10. They can hurt people physically and/or spiritually.
11. They fear Jesus and the name of Jesus.
12. They are spiritual beings.
13. They generally cannot be seen but the affects of their presence can be detected.
14. They have power only by God's permission.
15. They can manifest their presence in various ways, such as speaking out of an individual or throwing a person indwelt by them into physical convulsions.

THE POWER OF OUR LORD-Mark 1:21-45

Lessons about THE POWER OF OUR LORD from the evidence of that power operative as recorded in Mark 1:21-45

1. The power of our Lord is always capable of handling any need of any kind.
2. It operates always on the basis of God's grace alone.
3. It does not need a larger audience around to achieve miracles.
4. It is not limited for its operation to any one location.
5. It is completely effective in the healing of physical sickness or the casting out of demons.
6. It is needed by people with all sorts of problems.

7. It can be exercised in answer to importunate prayer. (See Mark 1:40)
8. It can be experienced as healing power in various ways, for example by just Jesus' spoken word (Mark 1:25), by taking the sick person's hand (Mark 1:31) or by a touch and the spoken word. (Mark 1:41)
9. It can achieve results that will anger and astound numbers of people. (See Mark 1:27)
10. It should cause people to seek out Jesus for help with their needs. (See Mark 1:37 especially)

DIVINE HEALING-Mark 1:29-45

Lessons about DIVINE HEALING from the Lord's healings recorded in Mark 1:29-45

1. Divine healing can be required in the physical or spiritual realm.
2. It can be handled by Jesus adequately, completely and successfully.
3. It is never too much for our Lord to handle.
4. It will always be carried out well by our Lord.
5. It requires that those who need it come to Jesus with the requests. (See James 4:2b)
6. It demands faith in our Lord's healing ability. (See Mark 1:40 "If you are willing, you can...")
7. It is not limited to a certain place. (It can occur in a home or out on a roadway.)
8. It can take place to enable a person to give immediate and additional service. (See Mark 1:31 "The fever left her and she waited on them.")
9. It expects the obedience of the Lord's commands from the person healed. (See Mark 1:41-45)
10. It is a reality to be relied upon in faith in times of severe need for God's help.

POPULARITY WITH PEOPLE-Mark 1:32-39

Lessons about POPULARITY WITH PEOPLE from the popularity Jesus had with the general populace of His day as recorded in Mark 1:32-39

1. Popularity with people can be very fleeting.
2. It can create hindrances to one's ministry.
3. It can make it almost impossible for a person to have quiet times with the Lord.
4. It can require service at all hours of the day or the evening, if we let it.
5. It can open up opportunities for ministry which others do not have.
6. It can result in crowds getting the help Jesus has to give them.
7. It can be expected from some people and not others. (Here: the Pharisees, for example)

OUR LORD-Mark 2

Lessons about OUR LORD from His presence in Mark 2

1. Our Lord has answers for the problems in people's lives.
2. He knows the thoughts in people's minds without their expressing them audibly.
3. He knows the Scriptures and can cite them immediately in His conversation when such references are needed. (See Mark 2:25-26)
4. He came not primarily for the righteous but for sinners.
5. He was popular and personable.
6. He was not fearful of criticism from critics.
7. He can command authoritatively; and when He does, He expects obedience. (For example, see Mark 2:14)
8. He always answers questions appropriately.
9. He is a good example of how to react to one's critics.
10. He has a place in His service for people for whom there may be no place elsewhere to serve. (e.g. Matthew, the tax collector)

THE LORD'S FORGIVENESS-Mark 2:1-12

Lessons on THE LORD'S FORGIVENESS OF SINS from His forgiveness of the sins of the paralytic written about it in Mark 2:1-12

1. The Lord's forgiveness of sins may be needed by people but not realized as a need at first.
2. It may be the most crucial need a person has, definitely more important than any physical needs.
3. It can be had for the taking by faith.
4. It can be granted by the Lord Himself and Him only.
5. It is a healing, as real as any physical healing that may take place, even though it be unseen.

BRINGING PEOPLE TO JESUS FOR HELP-Mark 2:1-12

Lessons on BRINGING PEOPLE TO JESUS FOR HELP from the bringing of the paralytic to Jesus by his four friends recorded in Mark 2:1-12

1. Bringing people to Jesus for help may demand unusual and unique ways of doing it.
2. It will often demand the cooperation of several people to be successful.
3. It may also be criticized.
4. It may be difficult on occasion and almost seemingly impossible. (It had been said, "Where there is a will there is a way." Note the difficulties to be overcome here by the four men: the crowd in the home, the popularity of Jesus that caused it, the presence of critics, and the fear of public opposition.)
5. It can often demand great sacrifice of time and effort.
6. It is a need so important that we ought to use any legitimate means possible to succeed in making it happen.

FASTING-Mark 2:18-22

Lessons about FASTING from the Lord's teaching regarding it in Mark 2:18-22

1. Fasting is a legitimate biblical practice on certain occasions.
2. It can be but should not be practiced only for "show."
3. It can be a sign of deep sorrow done in humility on occasion.
4. It has a proper time, place and purpose.

5. It should be practiced for right motives, never to be seen or praised by onlookers. (See also Matthew 6:16-18)
6. It should not be a cause for pride in the one fasting.
7. It is a personal matter and should not be legislated for or imposed on someone by another person.

WORKING SIX DAYS AND RESTING ON A SEVENTH DAY-Mark 2:23-3:6

Lessons about WORKING SIX DAYS AND RESTING ON A SEVENTH DAY, commonly called the Lord's day, from Jesus' teaching on the Sabbath in Mark 2:23-3:6

Introductory notes about "the Lord's Day"

1. The principle of working six days and resting on a seventh day was established by God at creation. (See Genesis 2:1-3)
2. The one of the Ten Commandments not repeated in the New Testament is the fourth one about remembering the Sabbath day to keep it holy. (See Exodus 20:8-11)
3. All of the other nine commandments are in the New Testament either in quotes or in inferences.
4. The reason may be because the Lord knew the day of rest would change for the church from the seventh (Saturday) to the first day of the week (Sunday). (See I Corinthians 16:1-2, for example)
5. According to the principle established at creation, those who must work on the day normally given for "rest" would obviously need to take another day to give their bodies and minds relaxation. (e.g. the Levites and priests, ministers, etc.)

Lessons about THE LORD'S DAY from Mark 2:23-3:6

1. The Lord's Day has been established by the Lord for the good of mankind.
2. It is to be a day of rest, relaxation and change from the work of the other six days.
3. It should be a different day from the other six days of the week.

4. It is under the sovereign control of the Lord Himself.
5. It should be a day of freedom from the usual responsibilities of the week which are to be given up for one day.
6. It is not meant to prevent the carrying out of legitimate human duties that must be carried out daily without exception. (e.g. the preparation of food, the ministry to patients in the hospital, the doing of legitimate farm chores, the ministry to those in emergencies, etc.)
7. It is a day when works of necessity and works of mercy shown to others can and should be done without violating the sanctity or purpose of the day.

PEOPLE WHO JESUS HELPS-Mark 3:1-19

Lessons about PEOPLE WHO GET HELP FROM JESUS from those He helped described in Mark 3:1-19

1. People who get help from Jesus are people with all kinds of problems, physical and spiritual.
2. They will be able to get help from Jesus, no matter what the problem, if they seek for it from Him.
3. They ought to be able to get help from Him especially in a place of worship, no matter what the day on which they come.
4. They cannot always pick the day on which they can come to be healed.
5. They will have to get Jesus' help when He is available.
6. They are always welcomed by Jesus.
7. They are never so much in need that He cannot help them.
8. They can come from all nationalities and be assured of a welcome from our Lord.
9. They can be so multitudinous that Jesus needs helpers to aid Him in His ministry.
10. They may come to Jesus in large groups but Jesus deals with each needy person as a seeking individual. (Here: Mark 3:1 "A man with a withered hand")

RELATIVES AND THEIR POSSIBLE MISUNDERSTANDING OF OUR MISSION- Mark 3:20-21

Lessons about RELATIVES AND THEIR POSSIBLE MISUNDERSTANDING OF OUR MISSION from Jesus' kinsmen and their misunderstanding of His mission as pictured in Mark 3:20-21 (Compare Mark 3:31-35)

1. Relatives can easily misunderstand the Christian, especially if they are not believers themselves.
2. They can try to dissuade the Christian from his or her ministry.
3. They may even be antagonistic to one's continuance in the Lord's work.
4. They can try to hinder one's usefulness to the Lord.
5. They can be so wrong at times and even for the best of motives.

THE UNPARDONABLE SIN-Mark 3:20-30

Lessons about THE UNPARDONABLE SIN from its description by Jesus given in Mark 3:20-30

1. The unpardonable sin is a very serious sin to be avoided at all costs.
2. It is an eternal sin which can never be forgiven.
3. It is a sin against the Holy Spirit, but not every sin against Him.
4. It is one of the sins of the tongue that reflects an evil heart attitude set firmly against the Spirit's leading. (Note Matthew 12:34 and Luke 6:45)
5. It is unpardonable because of the continuous sinning reflecting a continued hardness of heart. (See Hebrews 6:4-6 and 10:26-27)
6. It involves continued resistance to the gracious influences of the Holy Spirit by insuperable hardness and impenitence to the last.
7. It is a sin of the tongue, as will as a sin of the mind and of action.

THE MISUNDERSTANDING OF PEOPLE CONCERNING ONE'S WORK FOR THE LORD- Mark 3:20-34

Lessons about THE MISUNDERSTANDING OF PEOPLE CONCERNING ONE'S WORK FOR THE LORD from the misunderstanding of Jesus' work by His kinsmen and the scribes described in Mark 3:20-34

1. The misunderstanding of people concerning one's work for the Lord often happens to people whom God is using in some great way.
2. It often takes the form of severe vocal criticism.
3. It can come at times from those who should understand a person the best.
4. It may be best to ignore it or one may try to explain its unreasonableness. (See Mark 3:23-27)
5. It can hinder one from doing God's will, if he or she lets it.
6. It may require answering on occasion.
7. It ought to be handled calmly, peacefully, and reasonably, if it needs handling at all.
8. It may be caused by ignorance or jealousy.
9. It can ultimately result in a sin that is unpardonable. (See Mark 3:28-30)
10. It can result in very dangerous criticizing of the clear work of the Spirit of God.

SPIRITUAL KINSHIP TO JESUS-Mark 3:31-35

Lessons about SPIRITUAL KINSHIP TO JESUS from Jesus' remarks about it in Mark 3:31-35 (Compare Mark 3:20-21)

1. Spiritual kinship to Jesus is reflected in living according to God's will.
2. It is very important to our eternal welfare.
3. It is based on our regulation of our lives by God's will as revealed in the Bible.
4. It can be recognized by others who know their Bibles.

5. It can be recognized by others because there will be a "family" resemblance.
6. It is often a closer relationship than any physical family ties.
7. It is based on an implicit faith in the Lord's Word that is reflected in our obedience.
8. It should take precedence over physical kinship when the two may seem to conflict.
9. It may be so close and extremely important on occasion that it almost makes Christians look like they are ignoring their physical relations and not even caring about them.
10. It is very important for the continuation of the Lord's work.

ANGER-Mark 3:5

Lessons about ANGER from the anger of the Lord as He looked around with anger on the critical Pharisees as described in Mark 3:5

1. Anger is not always wrong and sinful. (See Ephesians 4:26-27) However, it can often be sinful as described in the Bible elsewhere. (For example, see Ephesians 4:31 and Colossians 3:8)
2. It can, on occasion, be described as righteous indignation.
3. It can be caused by a desire to defend God and His purposes.
4. It can arise out of personal distress over wrongs done to God and others by sinners with hardened hearts.
5. It is a legitimate emotion which a person can feel.

THE WORD OF GOD-Mark 4:1-20

Lessons about THE WORD OF GOD from the parable of the sower told by Jesus in Mark 4:1-20

1. The Word of God bears fruit in the lives of hearers, if they let it.
2. It can be choked out by the worries and cares of this life.

3. It can be stolen from our lives by Satan in various ways.
4. It demands broadcasting by the people who have it and believe it.
5. It is not equally successful in all lives.
6. It will vary in fruitfulness depending upon the conditions of the hearts of the people to whom it comes.
7. It needs to gain deep root in the lives of people in order to be effective in providing fruit.
8. It can have varying effects even in the lives of believers who accept it. (See Mark 3:20)
9. It can have temporary success in lives which will not last under affliction and persecution.
10. It is intended to have a permanent lodging and a fruitful effect in the lives of its hearers.

THE CHRISTIAN LIFE-Mark 4:1-20

Lessons on THE CHRISTIAN LIFE from the parable of the sower recorded in Mark 4:1-20

1. The Christian life is a battle for spiritual lives.
2. It is nourished by the teaching of the Word.
3. It can be lost or forfeited by carelessness.
4. It can become choked out by the affairs of this life.
5. It thrives on the Word of God that is accepted into the hearts of hearers and believers.
6. It should lead to fruitfulness in terms of life and converts.
7. It must be retained and maintained at all costs.
8. It will involve attacks from Satan.
9. It can produce fruit, more fruit and much fruit.

THE PRESENTATION OF THE WORD OF GOD-Mark 4:1-20

Lessons on THE PRESENTATION OF THE WORD OF GOD from the way Jesus did it recorded in Mark 4:1-20

1. The presentation of the Word of God should be done broadly and widely to as many people as possible.

2. It may be done with the help of parables and other kinds of analogies.
3. It can be done in various locations, such as teaching by a lakeside from a boat, instead of inside a building.
4. It should begin where people are in their knowledge of it, to take them where they are not but where you want them to be.
5. It can use common and ordinary illustrations.
6. It will not be received by some people.
7. It will be received very superficially by others.
8. It will be hindered by Satan by any means he can use.

PROBLEMS IN LIFE-Mark 4:38-41

Lessons about PROBLEMS IN LIFE from the storm on the Sea of Galilee recorded in Mark 4:38-41

1. Problems in life will always be with us in this life.
2. They should never cause us to forget that the Lord is in control of all circumstances.
3. They may come unexpectedly.
4. They will test our faith and demand faith.
5. They will not always be solved the way we think they should be; but we may be sure that the grace to face the problem will be given us.
6. They are often intensified by our not taking them immediately to the Lord in prayer.
7. They are never problems too great for the Lord to handle.
8. They are allowed for a purpose.
9. They can come to those doing what the Lord has commanded them to do.
10. They can be calmed by just a word from the Lord.

SERVICE FOR THE LORD-Mark 6:1-6

Lessons to learn about SERVICE FOR THE LORD from the Lord's ministry in Nazareth described in Mark 6:1-6

1. Service for the Lord will succeed when the messenger is respected and trusted by those who hear him or her.
2. It is hindered severely by unbelief. (See Mark 6:5)

3. It can be tough in one's own hometown where one is known long and well.
4. It should be practical in that it results in help to people with all sorts of problems.
5. It can result in miracles happening or questions of doubt coming from unbelieving hearts.

UNBELIEF-Mark 6:1-6

Lessons about UNBELIEF from the description of the Lord's ministry in the synagogue in Nazareth in Mark 6:1-6

1. Unbelief makes great and many miracles impossible.
2. It can be so great it even amazes the Lord. (See Mark 6:6)
3. It can keep people from being healed.
4. It often is seen in relatives of the teacher and people living in his or her hometown.
5. It causes people to look at things naturally, how they appear on the surface.
6. It makes it hard for God's work to prosper.

TELLING THE TRUTH-Mark 6:14-29

Lessons on TELLING THE TRUTH from John's declaring of the truth recorded in Mark 6:14-29

1. Telling the truth can cost persons dearly, even their very lives.
2. It must be told, sometimes in spite of the suffering it may bring to the teller.
3. It can mean calling sin "sin."
4. It should be backed up by the lives of those who tell it. (See Mark 6:20)
5. It should be a characteristic of the speech of Christians, no matter what the consequences. (See Matthew 6:33) "If a person lies to me once, I don't know when I can trust that person, if he tells me the truth a thousand times."

SIN-Mark 6:14-29

Lessons on SIN from the sin of Herod and Herodias described in Mark 6:14-29

1. Sin can take many forms.
2. It can result in terrible consequences.
3. It can be inspired by wicked people who hold grudges.
4. It should never be committed, no matter what the circumstances.
5. It cannot be run from or hidden indefinitely.

Barclay Commentary: The trouble with Herodias was that she wished to eliminate the one man who had the courage to confront her with her sin. She wished to do as she liked with no one to remind her of the moral law. She murdered John that she might sin in peace. She forgot that she need no longer meet John, but that she still had to meet God.

MEETING NEEDS OF PEOPLE-Mark 6:30-44

Lessons on MEETING THE NEEDS OF PEOPLE from the Lord's doing of it here as recorded in Mark 6:30-44

1. Meeting the needs of people should always bring glory to God, never to the doer of the deeds.
2. It should be done in an orderly, systematic way.
3. It is a major reason for our being on earth.
4. It can demonstrate God's great power and ability.
5. It is a major interest of the Lord.
6. It grows out of its compassion for others and should be a compelling reason for our service as well.
7. It may involve physical needs, as well as spiritual.
8. It is something that the disciples of the Lord should always be interested in doing.
9. It should take priority even over physical rest for the body. (See Mark 6:31-34)
10. It will often require the use of provisions at hand, no matter how insufficient they may seem.

SERVICE FOR THE LORD-Mark 6:30-44

Lessons on SERVICE FOR THE LORD from the service given the Lord by the disciples as recorded in Mark 6:30-44

1. Service for the Lord will demand that we serve other people.
2. It can require the ignoring of your own needs, even for rest, as you serve the needs of others.
3. It should be a major goal in life.
4. It will often require implicit dependence on the Lord.
5. It will require helping others and serving other people.
6. It may require a sacrifice of time, energy, and supplies.
7. It can be very exciting as we watch Him work through us.
8. It can be carried out continuously without any rest or with very little rest at times.
9. It will depend always on the person and the power of the Lord for success.
10. It should be carried out in an orderly fashion.

FAITH IN THE LORD-Mark 6:30-44

Lessons regarding FAITH IN THE LORD from the faith in the Lord of the disciples demonstrated here in Mark 6:30-44

1. Faith in the Lord will often demand that we go directly against reason and expect the unreasonable.
2. It always will show itself in actions of obedience.
3. It is required for miracles to happen.
4. It will overlook the natural as it expects the miraculous and the impossible.
5. It often demands that we do what we can with the expectation that the Lord will do what we cannot.

MATERIAL NEEDS OF PEOPLE-Mark 6:30-44

Lessons regarding MATERIAL NEEDS OF PEOPLE from the needs of the crowd recorded in Mark 6:30-44

1. Material needs of people are understood by the Lord and are of concern to Him.

2. They can be met by the Lord, no matter how serious or overwhelming they may be.
3. They may be met by the Lord through the use of His people.
4. They may not be met luxuriously but always sufficiently (no dessert but twelve baskets of food left over).
5. They may be brought into our lives to teach us that the Lord is interested in our material needs, as well as our spiritual.
Appendix: Little is much when God is in it.

OBEDIENCE TO JESUS-Mark 6:30-49

Lessons on OBEDIENCE TO JESUS from the obedience of the disciples and the crowd recorded in Mark 6:30-49

1. Obedience to Jesus should be given without any hesitation or questioning at all.
2. It is commanded and expected by the Lord.
3. It will always result in good things happening for the ones who obey.
4. It should stem from the faith that the Lord knows what He is doing, even if we cannot understand it.
5. It can require sacrifice on our parts.
6. It should be granted with trust in the Lord without doubt or complaint.
7. It can achieve miracles that are unbelievable.
8. It is necessary if Jesus is to minister to the multitudes with needs.
9. It may seem useless and even stupid at times from the natural vantage point.
10. It is important at all times, but especially in times of critical need.

PRAYER-Mark 6:45, 46

Lessons regarding PRAYER from Jesus' practice recorded in Mark 6:45, 46

1. Prayer is a good practice when the problems are coming fast and our ministry is very tiring.

2. It sometimes demands some quiet time with the Lord.
3. It is important for all of us if it was important for Jesus, the Son of God.
4. It may follow a great miracle (as well as precede it).
5. It may require hours of time. (He could see his disciples struggling on the lake in the storm about 3 A.M. See Mark 6:48)
6. It should be left and other action be taken on occasion.
7. It will often demand our leaving of the crowds.
8. It can be refreshing after a time of ministry for the Lord.
9. It may demand some privacy.
10. It is more important, on occasion, than public ministry. Conclusion: They thought, because they couldn't see him, He couldn't see them.

TROUBLE FOR CHRISTIANS-Mark 6:45-52

Lessons regarding TROUBLE FOR CHRISTIANS from the trouble the disciples experienced on the Sea of Galilee recorded in Mark 6:45-52

1. Trouble for Christians can come for all kinds of reasons, many of them divinely good ones.
2. It can come when we are doing what the Lord wants us to do.
3. It can be so severe that we despair of life itself.
4. It can cause us to think that the Lord does not know about it and even that He does not care about us.
5. It can never be too difficult for the Lord to handle.
6. It can be so severe that it causes us to forget the miracles of even the recent past. (See Mark 6:48)
7. It is known by the Lord and has His sympathy and concern.
8. It will demand that we do what we can do. (See Mark 6:48)
9. It will often get worse before it gets better. (See Mark 6:49, 50)
10. It can become an opportunity for the Lord to demonstrate power. (See Mark 6:52, see also John 6:21) Appendix: They must have thought because they could not see the Lord, He could not see them. How foolish! (See Mark 6:46, 47)

38

FEAR-Mark 6:45-52

Lessons regarding FEAR from the fear of the disciples on the Sea of Galilee recorded in Mark 6:45-52

1. Fear can come on us very suddenly and unexpectedly.
2. It is often caused by experiences for which we are not prepared.
3. It can come because we think we are absent from the Lord or we think that the Lord does not care about us.
4. It can cause us to forget, at least for the moment, the precious miracles that the Lord has performed in our midst. (See Mark 6:52)
5. It demonstrates a lack of faith in the Lord's ability to take care of the fearful circumstances in our lives.

SERVING THE LORD-Mark 6:7-13

Lessons on SERVING THE LORD from the service for the Lord assigned to the twelve disciples recorded in Mark 6:7-13

1. Serving the Lord should be done at every available opportunity.
2. It must communicate the truth, no matter whether it is accepted by faith or not.
3. It takes great courage at times.
4. It should aim to achieve repentance on the part of the hearers.
5. It is often accompanied by miracles.
6. It should result in help for people, both physically and spiritually.
7. It brings liberation of various kinds to those to whom one ministers.
8. It involves the offering of mercy as well as the warning of judgment.
9. It can involve the preaching of repentance, a message that does not originate with the preacher but with the Lord.
10. It can have encouraging results or discouraging ones.

MORAL UNCLEANNESS-Mark 7:1-23

Lessons on MORAL UNCLEANNESS from Mark 7:1-23

1. Moral uncleanness comes from inside a person.
2. It is more important in God's sight than the ritual or physical kinds.
3. It results in all kinds of unclean attitudes and actions.
4. It is to be shunned by the child of God.
5. It is not washed off by a ritual bath or hand-washing with water.

Keep your heart with all diligence so that nothing may enter therein and nothing may go out there from that is not right, holy, and pure.

Attitudes AND ACTIONS are important before God.

GOD'S COMMANDMENTS-Mark 7:1-23

Lessons about GOD'S COMMANDMENTS from Mark 7:1-23

1. God's commandments must not be set aside by man's commandments, the traditions of mankind.
2. They are given to help a person live a clean life before God.
3. They can relate to moral issues and often do.
4. They are important.
5. They are always broken at a person's own risk.

HELP FROM THE LORD-Mark 7:24-36

Lessons in HELP FROM THE LORD from Mark 7:24-36

1. Help from the Lord is available for both men and women.
2. It is available for the asking and comes in response to faith.
3. It is available for all ages.
4. It is available for physical and spiritual healing.
5. It may come in ways that test our faith.

FAITH-Mark 7:24-36

Lessons on FAITH from Mark 7:24-36

1. Faith may be exercised on behalf of other people, some who possibly cannot exercise it for themselves.
2. It is expected by the Lord and is rewarded by Him.
3. It is evidenced by action. (Note: The woman went when Jesus told her to do so and did not stay, begging for a sign.)
4. It may be tested by the Lord before He grants our requests. (See Mark 7:27-29)
5. It can achieve the supernatural.
6. It can bring spiritual healing (the daughter) or physical healing (the man).
7. It may seemingly receive a "no" answer but this need not be final as the believer perseveres in prayer.
8. It is a very real entity.
9. It must be lodged firmly in a promise from God to succeed. (See Mark 7:29)
10. It can be exercised by Jews or Gentiles and be rewarded for either with great miraculous answers.

THE LORD'S WORK-Mark 7:24-26

Lessons about THE LORD'S WORK from Mark 7:24-26

1. The Lord's work regularly involves helping people.
2. It can be received by prayer for help.
3. It may demand the use of means or help can be granted by just a spoken word.
4. It is always done well and completely.
5. It is often needed because problems people have cannot be handled by the natural means available.

INTERCESSION-Mark 7:24-36

Lessons about INTERCESSION from Mark 7:24-36

1. Intercession is important if we are to get help from the Lord for other people.
2. It is type of prayer offered on behalf of other people and their needs.

3. It can achieve the supernatural and the miraculous even for persons who are not present.
4. It may be offered on behalf of a relative, a friend or even a stranger.
5. It regularly takes time and effort away from other things that are considered of less importance at the time.

PARENTS-Mark 7:8-13

Lessons about PARENTS from Mark 7:8-13

1. Parents are to be respected by their children.
2. They are not to be evil spoken of by their children.
3. They should be supported by their children when the children are able to do so and their parents need help.
4. They are to be honored according to one of the Ten Commandments.
5. They should be honored all their lives, obeyed while at home, and supported as needs arise.

PROBLEMS-Mark 8:1-10

Lessons about PROBLEMS from the problem regarding food

described in Mark 8:1-10

1. Problems are part of life for everyone here on planet earth.
2. They are never more than the Lord can handle.
3. They may require a miracle as a solution.
4. They may not take much to solve them when the Lord is around and working.
5. They may relate to a lack of physical resources.
6. They will often seem insurmountable with the physical resources at hand.
7. They should be brought immediately to the Lord in urgent prayer.
8. They must be brought in faith that the Lord can undertake for them.
9. They can (and will, if it is His will) be handled by the Lord in a more than merely adequate way. (See Mark 8:8)

10. They can be problems that affect us in many ways, including the physical.

MIRACLES-Mark 8:1-10, 14-21

Lessons about MIRACLES from Jesus' feeding the four thousand recorded in Mark 8:1-10, 14-21

1. Miracles can be expected when we are on the Lord's side and He is with us to provide.
2. They can be expected whenever God's children need them.
3. They always require faith in the Lord's ability.
4. They always require that we do what we can do first.
5. They are dependent upon obedience to the Lord's commands.

FAITH IN CHRIST-Mark 8:22-38

Lessons on FAITH IN CHRIST from the events of Mark 8:22-38

1. Faith in Christ must be implicit for healing or help from the Lord.
2. It must accept Him at His Word implicitly.
3. It may be resident in intercessors for another individual's healing. (See Mark 8:22)
4. It is important for divine help but so also is faith that Jesus is who He claims to be. (See Mark 8:29)
5. It is a conviction that what is impossible with man is completely possible with God.

DISCIPLESHIP-Mark 8:31-38

Lessons on DISCIPLESHIP from Jesus' teaching in Mark 8:31-38

1. Discipleship will bring some great surprises to us. (The Lord does things differently quite often.)
2. It will demand that all we have be given to the Lord.
3. It will demand great faith in the Lord and trust in His Word.
4. It will demand a resolute selling out of self and a selling out to the Lord.

43

5. It will demand a continuous following of the Lord's teaching. (See Mark 8:34)
6. It will demand a fearless witness for Christ.
7. It demands a correct concept of who Jesus is, not only just a faith in Him. ("Who do you say I am?")
8. It should be accepted without fear or shame.
9. It can demand giving up real living now for real living later.
10. It can demand the ultimate sacrifice of a disciple's life.

OBEDIENCE-Mark 8:31-38

Lessons on OBEDIENCE from Jesus' teaching in Mark 8:31-38

1. Obedience should continue on the part of every Christian.
2. It is expected by Jesus of all His disciples.
   • Mark 8:25 "Don't go into the village."
   • Mark 8:30 "Don't tell anyone about me."
   • Mark :34 "Deny yourself, take up your cross, and continue following me."
3. It is a sign of a true disciple.
4. It is an indication of gratitude to God.
5. It involves always thinking "What does God think about this?" and then a doing of His will.

IMPORTANT SPIRITUAL EXPERIENCES IN LIFE-Mark 9:1-13

Lessons regarding IMPORTANT SPIRITUAL EXPERIENCES IN LIFE from the experience of the disciples on the Mount of Transfiguration recorded in Mark 9:1-13

1. Important spiritual experiences in life come to prepare us for service and other experiences ahead.
2. They come often to a select few who stay close to Jesus.
3. They come for those who are prepared for them.
4. They can come at surprising times and in surprising places.
5. They must not be clung to or selfishly kept to oneself.
6. They come for various purposes.

7. They can help us over the rough spots which often come later in life as one recalls them.
8. They come to pass.
9. They come for encouragement.
10. They can bring us additional light from the Lord, light in which He expects us to walk. (See Mark 9:7 "This is my beloved Son. Keep on listening to Him.")

PROBLEMS IN LIFE-Mark 9:14-32

Lessons about PROBLEMS IN LIFE from the problems of the demon-possessed boy needing correction here as described in Mark 9:14-32

1. Problems in life can be so severe that only Jesus can handle them.
2. They often face us after high spiritual experiences.
3. They can demand a miracle if they are to be corrected.
4. They demand faith in the Lord's ability to handle any problem.
5. They can be handled by one person's intercession for another, maybe one who cannot intercede for himself or herself.
6. They demand that a person be prayed up if he or she is to be of help in some situations.
7. They may appear at first to get worse before they get better. (See Mark 9:25- 26)
8. They demand faith in the Lord on the part of the pray-er if they are to be taken care of successfully. (See Mark 9:24)
9. They can be great teaching opportunities. (See Mark 9:28- 29)
10. They can be life-threatening and demanding of immediate attention. (See Mark 9:18, 20, 22, 26)
11. They can be problems which have existed for a long time. (See Mark 9:21)
12. They can be impossible for some people to handle for various reasons.

13. They can be successfully handled by one person when a number of people (disciples in Mark 9:18) may have tried and been unsuccessful.
14. They can seem so simple for our Lord to handle when they are turned over to Him. (See Mark 9:25-27)
15. They need not be causes for distress and alarm for all those who believe. (See Mark 9:23)

MARRIAGE-Mark 10:1-12

Lessons about MARRIAGE from Jesus' teaching on marriage recorded in Mark 10:1-12

1. Marriage was intended to be monogamous from the beginning.
2. It was an institution initiated by God.
3. It demands leaving other relationships for the closest relationship on the earthly level.
4. It involves a very close union as God looks at it.
5. It cannot be dissolved for any reason according to this passage. (See Matthew 5:32 and 19:9)
6. It is to be a life-long, permanent union.
7. It is for better or worse, whatever either of those may involve.
8. It involves a man and a woman who want to and vow to live together.
9. It is not to be a homosexual relationship. "male and female"
10. It is a very serious matter before God.
11. It does not necessarily have to follow any biblically prescribed "ceremony."
12. It is not to be entered into lightly or ill-advisedly.
13. It does not mean that a person should leave his or her parents in the lurch but only that he or she should not let a parental relationship take precedence over a marital one.
14. It is not to be separated by any outsider.
15. It is a serious relationship as God and His Word considers it.

CHRISTIAN DISCIPLESHIP-Mark 10:13-31

Lessons on CHRISTIAN DISCIPLESHIP from discipleship as seen in Mark 10:13-31

1. Christian discipleship demands sacrifice, sometimes everything a person has.
2. It is costly.
3. It requires putting the Lord first and everything else in life second.
4. It should be a natural outgrowth after receiving the Lord as Savior.
5. It is more than just keeping commandments.
6. It will demand being close to the Lord and living like He does.
7. It does consist of doing things as well as being something.
8. It demands spending yourself and your possessions for others.
9. It can mean the loss of home, family and friends.
10. It can mean an introduction into a far greater and wider family than one may have left.
11. It may not be an easy way but can be fraught with persecution.
12. It brings great rewards in the age to come.
13. It will involve one in doing good things for other people. (See Mark 10:21)

Note: The commandments that Jesus quoted are all but one negative. (Mark 10:14)

Note also that, in effect, the man's answer was saying, "I never in my life did anyone any harm." That may have been true, but the real question was, "what good had he done people?" Especially when he had tremendous wealth to do tremendous good for many. When the man went away grieved, he was saying "I want discipleship but not that much." A person must want Christianity badly enough to give his or her possessions away. A good question each of us should ask ourselves is "What on earth are we doing for heaven's sake?"

THE LORD-Mark 10:13-31

Lessons about THE LORD from his appearance in Mark 10:13-31

1. The Lord always has time for people, even the children.
2. He can be very demanding at times, but always loving.
3. He always tells things like they are.
4. He does not mince words.
5. He wants people to think as they come to Him. (This was the reason for His question to the man in Mark 10:18)

MATERIAL WEALTH-Mark 10:17-31

Lessons on MATERIAL WEALTH from the teaching of Jesus about wealth in Mark 10:17-31

1. Material wealth can so easily keep a person out of the kingdom of God.
2. It can cause one to become stingy and to hoard.
3. It is not necessarily sinful but is always dangerous.
4. It is often looked on as a sign of God's honor and blessing.
5. It tends to "fix a man's heart to this world." Barclay
6. It tends to make a man think of everything in terms of financial cost.
7. It can make a person forget the things money cannot buy.
8. It can make a person think that money can buy anything.
9. It is a great responsibility.
10. It can enable a person to do a lot of good for many people. (See Mark 10:21)

GREATNESS IN GOD'S KINGDOM-Mark 10:35-45

Lessons about GREATNESS IN GOD'S KINGDOM from the teaching of Jesus in Mark 10:35-45

1. Greatness in God's Kingdom is attained through suffering and service.

48

2. It is not Christ's to give to us.
3. It can be sought but must be sought in the right way.
4. It does not consist in how many people one controls.
5. It is not attained by special favor or arbitrary allotment.
6. It can demand a terrific price to be paid for it.
7. It is certainly something desirable to receive. (Compare Matthew 5:19)
8. It is achievable by the right kind of people.

SERVICE TO OTHERS-Mark 10:35-45

Lessons about SERVICE TO OTHERS from the teaching of Jesus in Mark 10:35-45

1. Service to others can involve even giving up one's life for others.
2. It is the sign of true greatness as far as heaven is concerned.
3. It is the purpose for which we are here.
4. It is expected of Christ's followers.
5. It can involve great suffering and sorrow.
6. It comes from true Christian modesty and humility.
7. It should be done out of gratitude for all Christ has given us.
8. It should arise out of a desire to follow the Lord's example. (See Mark 10:45)

SELF-SEEKING-Mark 10:35-45

Lessons about SELF-SEEKING from the self-seeking of James and John recorded in Mark 10:35-45

1. Self-seeking is regularly wrong.
2. It tends to separate friends from one another.
3. It often arouses discord among people and even indignation.
4. It has its source in selfishness.
5. It keeps us from our crosses.
6. It hurts the cause of Christ.
7. It is obnoxious when seen in other people.
8. It comes naturally to us as it is the core of all sinfulness.
9. It is the opposite of self-denial.

10. It often grows out of ignorance of all the facts. (See Mark 10:38-40)
11. It overlooks the fact that the great people among Jesus' followers are the servants of others.
12. It often leads one to overestimate his or her own abilities. (See Mark 10:39: "we are able.")

Appendix: A basic problem for us humans is that we wish to do as little as possible and still get as much as possible. (See William Barclay's comment on Mark 10:35-45)

THE LORD'S HELP-Mark 10:46-52

Lessons about THE LORD'S HELP from His help given to blind Bartimaeus in Mark 10:46-52

1. The Lord's help has to be wanted to be received.
2. It regularly comes in answer to believing prayer.
3. It is available for one (or many).
4. It is available for the believer.
5. It may come only after perseverance in crying for help.
6. It is given out of compassion for the person (or persons) suffering both physical and/or spiritual problems.

FAITH-Mark 10:46-52

Lessons on FAITH from the faith of blind Bartimaeus in Mark 10:46-52

1. Faith must show itself in action to achieve help.
2. It is always honored by the Lord.
3. It is the cry of a needy person for help.
4. It can enable a person to overcome hindrances in order to get to Jesus.
5. It will demonstrate itself in immediate actions of obedience.
6. It results in prayers being answered.
7. It believes God for the humanly impossible.
8. It can cause a person to rise above any obstacles to present his or her problem to Jesus.

9. It can result in immediate and complete answers from the Lord.

PRAYER-Mark 10:46-52

Lessons on PRAYER from the prayer of blind Bartimaeus in Mark 10:46-52

1. Prayer does not have to be long to be heard.
2. It is heard by the Lord.
3. It does not require any special language or vocabulary to gain the ear of the Lord.
4. It does not normally require any instruction but comes naturally from the needy heart.
5. It must grow out of faith if it is to succeed.
6. It demonstrates itself in desperate desire.
7. It should be as specific as the need.

THE COMMANDS OF JESUS-Mark 11:1-11

Lessons about THE COMMANDS OF JESUS given His disciples in Mark 11:1-11

1. The commands of Jesus may seem very strange indeed. (They were to take the colt and speak only if questioned)
2. They will work out in the end for our good, although they may seem foolish at the time.
3. They will demand faith on our part that the Lord knows what He is doing and asking.
4. They should be obeyed immediately and unquestioningly.
5. They will test our faith. (Other examples of things that may test us are: tithing, keeping the Lord's Day holy, etc.)
6. They are not always accompanied by reasons.
7. They often demand that we take one step at a time.
8. They grow out of His foreknowledge that all will work out in the end.
9. They are given with the expectation that they will be obeyed to the letter.

FAITH-Mark 11:20-25

Lessons on FAITH from Jesus' teaching on faith and believing in Mark 11:20-25

1. Faith is absolutely necessary for answers to prayer.
2. It is a virtue encouraged and praised by the Lord.
3. It implies we want God's help.
4. It is a secret of spiritual power.
5. It can relieve us of a load of care.
6. It can achieve what to the natural mind is impossible.

PRAYER-Mark 11:20-25

Lessons on PRAYER from Jesus' teaching on prayer in Mark 11:20-25

1. Prayer always gives God his rightful and proper place in our lives if it is prayed correctly.
2. It should be offered with the confidence that God can and does answer believing prayer.
3. It demands knowing what to pray for, and this comes from a thorough knowledge of God's Word.
4. It must include, either explicitly or implicitly, that the Lord's will be done if it is to be effective.
5. It will always get some kind of a response from God.
6. It should result in obedient action where such is demanded.
7. It is the means ordained by God whereby we get our needs taken care of.
8. It should be offered always with a pure heart and without any holding of grudges.
9. It can obtain the impossible.
10. It is the way to take our problems and difficulties to God.
11. It must be more than a mere formality.
12. It can be hindered by angry and uncharitable feelings.
13. It should be practiced by everyone in need.
14. It can change things.
15. It is a necessary practice for all of God's children.

GOD-Mark 12:1-12

Lessons about GOD from the owner of the vineyard, a type of God, in Mark 12:1-12

1. God is long-suffering to us, not willing that any should perish.
2. He does not like to punish but must on occasion when people have been unfaithful.
3. He is very generous. (Note: He gave the tenant farmers everything necessary to make their work easy and successful.)
4. He depends on people to do what He desires and this is never beyond their ability to accomplish. (Note: He went away and trusted the farmers to do the work well which they were supposed to do.)
5. He is patient with people. (Note: He gave them much time to pay what they owed him.)
6. He will triumph in the end always, even though people may take advantage of His patience.
7. He expects faithful work.
8. He depends on people to fulfill their obligations.
9. He has work to be doing which He has elected to have people accomplish for Him.
10. He will seek for others to work for him when some have proved unfaithful to their tasks.

CHRIST IN RELATION TO CHRISTIAN GIVING-Mark 12:41-44

Lessons about CHRIST IN RELATION TO CHRISTIAN GIVING as seen in the giving of the widow in Mark 12:41-44

1. Christ expects His people to give.
2. He observes the giving of His people.
3. He looks on some kinds of giving as worthy of higher praise than others.
4. He commends, relative to giving, what some people might call foolishness and wastefulness. ("She gave all she had.")

5. He praises her for what many would not expect, namely her loving sacrifice of herself in giving all she had to live on.
6. He is not embarrassed to talk about giving.
7. He does not look on our giving as people do so often.
8. He looks not so much at how much is given but at how much is left over after our giving.
9. He looks not only at what a person gives but also at what a persons keeps.
10. He looks more at the giver than at the gift.
11. He looks more at the attitude than at the amount, when it comes to the spiritual value and acceptability of our giving.
12. He looks more at the spirit with which we give than on the actual gifts themselves.
13. He expects our giving to bear some decent proportion to the good things He has given us. (See I Corinthians 16:2 "as God has prospered you" and II Corinthians 8:12 "according as what a person has, not according to what he or she doesn't have.")
14. He anticipates that our offerings will often involve sacrifice.
15. He recognizes that the Christian who gives trusts God to take care of any need his or her giving may cause.

DECEPTION-Mark 13

Lessons on DECEPTION from Jesus' teaching about the end times in Mark 13

1. Deception will intensify severely toward the end of the age.
2. It can affect even the Lord's disciples and may lead them astray.
3. It is something for which every Christian needs to be on the alert, lest he or she be misled into heresy.
4. It can come via false and deceptive words.
5. It can take the form of miracle-workings so as to attempt to lead astray even the very best people.
6. It can cause one to be unprepared for the return of his Lord.

7. It can be spiritually dangerous for one's soul.
8. It is something against which we definitely need to be warned.
9. It can be avoided by a person who has studied prophecy and is well grounded in the truth of God's Word.
10. It has its main goal to confuse people, Christian and non-Christian, and to get them to make wrong choices.

PERSECUTION FOR CHRIST-Mark 13:1-27

Lessons about PERSECUTION FOR CHRIST from the persecution described in Mark 13:1-27

1. Persecution for Christ will intensify as we approach the end of the age.
2. It can come even from one's own family members.
3. It can be very severe.
4. It is always controlled by our heavenly Father. (See Mark 13:20)
5. It may demand defense of ourselves verbally before courts.
6. It will bring with it the help of the Holy Spirit.
7. It can involve physical abuse and even mental torture.
8. It can come from both Jews and Gentiles.
9. It is always accompanied by divine help and strength.
10. It is to be expected by Christians who are living the Christian life the way it ought to be lived.

HATRED OF OTHERS-Mark 13:7-27

Lessons about HATRED OF OTHERS from the observations about it by Jesus in Mark 13:7-27

1. Hatred of others is a sin.
2. It can lead to doing terrible things to other people.
3. It will intensify toward the end of the age.
4. It can infect a person's own home and household. "Life becomes a hell upon earth when personal loyalties are destroyed and when there is no love a person can trust."
5. It can be caused by a hatred for Christ and righteous living by the Christian.

HERESY-Mark 13:7-27

Lessons about HERESY from the teaching of Christ in Mark 13:7-27

1. Heresy can arise because people want to construct doctrines to suit themselves rather than staying with what the Bible clearly teaches.
2. It can arise because of overemphasis on some doctrines to the exclusion of others.
3. It can come because of our attempt to produce a religion that is popular with people.
4. It will abound more and more in the last days.
5. It can easily infect us as we divorce ourselves from Christian fellowship.
6. It comes as a result of ignorance of God's Word or an ignoring of God's Word.

SERVICE FOR THE LORD-Mark 14:3-11

Lessons regarding SERVICE FOR THE LORD as seen in the woman's service to the Lord described in Mark 14:3-11

1. Service for the Lord should grow out of grateful love for Him.
2. It may seem wasteful of time, money and talents to some.
3. It sometimes has to be done immediately or the occasion for such service passes.
4. It can be done by women as well as men.
5. It may sometimes have to be done in the public eye.
6. It is always recognized somehow by the Lord.
7. It can express our deepest feelings for the Lord.
8. It can take various forms.
9. It can demand real humility and forgetfulness of self by the person doing it.
10. It may achieve more than the doer anticipates.

CENSORIOUS CRITICISM-Mark 14:3-11

Lessons regarding CENSORIOUS CRITICISM BY PEOPLE from the criticism of the woman's ministry to Jesus described in Mark 14:3-11

1. Criticism from others will often come if you are doing anything for the Lord.
2. It should be expected.
3. It can hurt people severely.
4. It is not constructive and can be quite discouraging.
5. It may come from the most surprising people. (Compare Matthew 26:8)
6. It can so often be started by one and infect others. (Compare Matthew 26:6-13; Mark 14:3-11; John 12:1-8)
7. It can be rebuked by a word from the Lord.
8. It is very unkind and unloving.
9. It can grow out of wrongful and selfish motives. (See John 12:6)

SACRIFICE-Mark 14:3-11

Lessons on SACRIFICE from the sacrifice of the woman described in Mark 14:3-11

1. Sacrifice will always cost us something.
2. It can be a sign of true love and devotion for the Lord.
3. It is always noticed by Him.
4. It can rise above considerations of thrift.
5. It may not seem the logical thing to do.
6. It often grows out of thoughtfulness for others.
7. It can seem like waste to less consecrated followers of the Lord.

OUR POSSESSIONS-Mark 14:3-11

Lessons on OUR POSSESSIONS from the woman's use of her perfume described in Mark 14:3-11

1. Our possessions should all be at the disposal of our Lord, no matter how expensive they may be.
2. They can make us greedy or generous.
3. They can possess us or we can possess them.

4. They can be used to show our commitment to the Lord.
5. They can be of various kinds, even some that one may might think could never be of any use to the Lord.

OVERCONFIDENCE-Mark 14:27-31

Lessons on OVERCONFIDENCE from the seeming overconfidence of Peter seen in Mark 14:27-31

1. Overconfidence can be very dangerous.
2. It can get a person into very "hot water."
3. It can be contagious.
4. It often shows itself in what one may say, not only in what one may do.
5. It can even cause a person, sometimes without even thinking, to contradict the explicit words of the Lord.

LIFE'S EMERGENCIES-Mark 14:32

Lessons about LIFE'S EMERGENCIES from the emergency Jesus faced in Gethsemane on Thursday night and on the Friday following as described in Mark 14:32 and following

1. Life's emergencies come even to those who are in the center of God's will.
2. They are part of life on planet earth.
3. They can be anticipated sometimes.
4. They demand prayerful preparation.
5. They can surprise us.
6. They can be extremely unpleasant.
7. They can be matters from which we pray for deliverance, although always with the condition that God's divine will be carried out above all else.

PRAYER-Mark 14:32-42

Lessons on PRAYER drawn from the praying of the Lord in the Garden of Gethsemane described in Mark 14:32-42.

1. Prayer is important in life but especially before crises of any kind.

2. It may be repeated for the same thing and even in the same words without it being a sign of unbelief before God on the part of the pray-er.
3. It should be addressed to the Father.
4. It can be tiring work if it is real.
5. It can cause one to grow weary.
6. It is not usually a successful practice for a drowsy person.
7. It can keep one from falling into temptation.
8. It is a practice that can be aided and encouraged by the presence (and even the participation) of others around.
9. It should be prayed with the idea always uppermost in mind that God's will be done, not ours.
10. It is a practice that should regularly characterize every child of God.

THE WILL OF THE LORD FOR OUR LIVES- Mark 14:34, 38

Lessons on THE WILL OF THE LORD FOR OUR LIVES from the will of the Lord for His disciples expressed to them in Mark 14:34, 38

1. The will of the Lord is not always what we most feel like doing.
2. It should have priority in our lives always.
3. It is often revealed to us very specifically. (e.g. Jesus to the disciples: "Watch and pray.")
4. It is not always easy to carry out. (They went to sleep.)
5. It must not be resisted for any reason.
6. It need not be understood to be accepted and carried out.
7. It is reasonable even though we may not know what His reasons are.

Luke

GOD'S WORD-Luke 1:1-38

Lessons about GOD'S WORD from His word to Zechariah and to Mary declared in Luke 1:1-38

1. God's Word can come via various ways. e.g. angels, a person, the written Word
2. It can be very specific.
3. It demands complete faith on the part of the receiver.
4. It is something God expects the receiver to believe and act on.
5. It can result in some dire consequences if it is not believed.

SUBMISSION TO GOD'S WILL-Luke 1:1-38

Lessons about SUBMISSION TO GOD'S WILL from that expected from Zechariah and Mary in Luke 1:1-38

1. Submission to God's will should be given immediately without questioning or hesitation.
2. It is expected by God of His own, especially of those who have walked with Him for some time.
3. It may not be understood at the time of submission.
4. It should involve our total being without reservations or conditions.
5. It can be painful, difficult, and cost one something.

ANSWERS TO PRAYER-Luke 1:13

Lessons on ANSWERS TO PRAYER from the answer to the prayer of Zechariah referred to in Luke 1:13

1. Answers to prayer come to the right king of people. (See James 5:16b)
2. They come in response to believing prayer.
3. They often come when we are busy about the work we should be doing.
4. They may be quite supernatural or more natural. (The angel was the supernatural part; the son was the normal route: sexual intercourse and a nine-month pregnancy.)

60

5. They come in God's own timing.
6. They often come in ways that astound us.
7. They should not startle us or surprise us.

PRAYER-Luke 1:5-25

Lessons about PRAYER from the prayer of Zachariah for a child as described in Luke 1:5-25. See especially Luke 1:13 where Gabriel says to Zachariah, "Your petition has been heard and your wife, Elizabeth, will bear you a son..."

1. Prayer should be offered about anything which is a burden.
2. It demands faith if it is to be heard.
3. It is heard sometimes in spite of a lack of faith on the part of the pray-er. (See Zechariah's question and remarks in Luke 1:18 and Gabriel's comments in Luke 1:19, 20)
4. It can be prayed for temporal needs, not just spiritual ones.
5. It often can and should be offered by husband and wife together, if possible.
6. It can achieve great miracles, but always in God's timing. (Here: They had been married a long time and had no son.)
7. It can and should be persevered in without it being a sign of a lack of faith.
8. It will be answered by God in some way. ("No" and "wait" are answers also.)
9. It is an important means ordained by God for obtaining what we need. (See James 4:20)
10. It may be offered for a long time before there is any indication that God has heard.

OUR GOD-Luke 1:5-25

Lessons about OUR GOD from His involvement in the birth of John in Luke 1:5-25

1. Our God answers prayer according to His own timetable.
2. He is all-powerful and nothing is too hard for him.

3. He can use angels to minister to the needs of His people to accomplish His purposes.
4. He loves surprises.
5. He is aware of what is going on down here on the earth and knows our needs before we ask Him. (See Matthew 6:8)
6. He does not appreciate unbelief in the lives of His people.
7. He will always carry out His promises to His people.
8. He has His own reasons for doing things the way He does them. (See Isaiah 55:8, 9)

UNBELIEF-Luke 1:5-25

Lessons on UNBELIEF from the unbelief of Zachariah seen in Luke 1:5-25, especially Luke 1:20

1. Unbelief displeases God, particularly when it is seen in older believers who should know better. (Compare Mary's question for information in Luke 1:34 and Gabriel's response.)
2. It can bring God's discipline and even judgment.
3. It can have lasting effects for some time. (e.g. Zachariah was unable to speak for nine months or more.)
4. It is sometimes an involuntary, sudden response to an almost unbelievable promise from God and as such is not a sin but only a temptation.
5. It should not be seen in God's children, especially in those who have followed Him for a long time.

GOD-Luke 1:26-45

Lessons about GOD from Luke 1:26-45

1. God is not limited to the ordinary ways of doing things.
2. He can do all things in keeping with His own nature.
3. He regularly does not override a person's free will. (Note: This does not involve a command to Mary but an announcement.)
4. He can use another person if His first choice is unusable for some reason.

5. He uses angels to do His bidding.
6. He faithfully fulfills the prophecies He has given before.

SUBMISSION TO THE KNOWN WILL OF GOD-Luke 1:26-45

Lessons about SUBMISSION TO THE KNOWN WILL OF GOD from Mary's submission seen in Luke 1:26-45

1. Submission to God's known will should be granted immediately without any strings attached and even without a full understanding.
2. It should involve our total being without reservation.
3. It can be made with complete trust in God's love, goodness, and wisdom.
4. It may not be understood at the time of submission.
5. It is expected even before additional specific light from God comes.

BELIEVERS-Luke 1:26-45

Lessons about BELIEVERS from Mary, a great believer, as seen in Luke 1:26-45

1. Believers will take God's Word for what it says.
2. They may question because of a lack of knowledge or information but not because of a lack of faith.
3. They will submit to God's will cheerfully and quickly on the spot.
4. They will be given special blessings by God.
5. They will put their reputation and even lives on the line for God.
6. They trust God that His will is always best.
7. They will give their bodies to God unreservedly for His use, no matter how, where or when He may use them.
8. They can be relatively young people of humble origin.
9. They can be and should be thinking people. vv. 29, 34
10. They will not let their brains stand in the way of their accepting and doing God's will.
11. They will accept God's will without excitement or alarm.
12. They believe that with God nothing is impossible.

13. They will accept situations from God that involve risks. (e.g. Peter getting out of the boat)
14. They will often demonstrate great courage on their parts.
15. They may have to wait for God's will to be carried out.
16. They may receive encouragement from talking with other believers for whom God has done great things. (e.g. Elizabeth)
17. They will not attach conditions to their commitment to God's will. (Conditions such as: if you tell me what you are going to do with my body; if you tell Joseph what is happening; if you give me time to think; etc.)
18. They take the Lord at His Word.
19. They may question God for understanding.
20. They have servant's hearts.
21. They have obedient hearts.
22. They are confident that God's will will be carried out.
23. They believe that impossibilities can be realized with God's help.
24. They need not worry about circumstances.
25. They can and do share God's blessings with other believers.
26. They will often gain confirmation and affirmation from other believers.
27. They have a strong desire to please God.
28. They will not doubt that God's will will be carried out but may only be inquiring how it will be carried out. (Was Mary to go on with her marriage to Joseph or was she to wait?)

GOD'S WILL FOR INDIVIDUALS-Luke 1:26-48

Lessons about GOD'S WILL FOR INDIVIDUALS from His will made known to Mary here in Luke 1:26-48

1. God's will for individuals often demands tremendous faith in God's Word and His power to do the miraculous.
2. It is not always the easiest thing to accept and to submit to.
3. It often affects other lives besides the life of the initial recipient. (e.g. Joseph)

4. It can affect one's future in large and miraculous ways.
5. It expects immediate acceptance and obedience without hesitation.
6. It is expected to be accepted without much thought when it is made clear to the receiver.
7. It can be very specifically revealed along with answers to questions requesting information.
8. It is always intended for our own best interests and often for the best interest of others in the long run.
9. It may trouble us when it is first revealed to us.
10. It is not always what we might choose for ourselves with our own limited knowledge.
11. It may be revealed to us alone and no one else, at least at first.
12. It is often unique and adapted to one individual alone.
13. It may not always be understood at the time.
14. It may seem foolish and even impossible from the situation as it stands at the time.
15. It may be revealed in normal or unusual ways.
16. It may demand a launching out in faith that God knows best.
17. It will involve often the use of means, often people, especially totally dedicated ones.
18. It should take precedence over our own wills.
19. It will not always be the easiest thing we ever did.
20. It is rarely revealed to us all at one time.
21. It often demands that we leave our "comfort zone."
22. It often demands that we trust Him totally to take care of unforeseen and unknown difficulties that may arise.
23. It can result in some wonderful surprises.
24. It will always be for our own long-range benefit, and often the good of many others as well.
25. It will always be what we would will for ourselves if we had all the information He has at our disposal.
26. It will never be more than we can handle with His help. (Note Gabriel's statement in Luke 1:37)
27. It may overwhelm us at first. (Note Mary's question)
28. It can affect our entire life.
29. It may complicate our lives.

FAITH IN GOD'S WORD-Luke 1:36-38

Lessons on FAITH IN GOD'S WORD from Mary the mother of Jesus seen in Luke 1:36-38

1. Faith in God's Word can be seen in the most surprising people.
2. It is not an exclusive possession of older folks.
3. It will lead a person to make a total commitment of oneself to God in advance of light received.
4. It can include trusting God with one's entire life and reputation.
5. It will include our total commitment of our bodies to God for His use. (See Romans 12:1)
6. It will cause the believer to respond positively and immediately to God's will, once it is known.
7. It makes the impossible possible.
8. It can mean severe sacrifices in one's life. (e.g. Mary's sacrifice of reputation, future plans, engagement, physical comfort, etc.)
9. It allows for sincere and honest questioning.
10. It will bring an answer from God and/or His servant.
11. It accepts the fact that our God can carry out what He has promised, no matter how miraculous.

GOD'S GUIDANCE FOR US-Luke 2:1-20

Lessons about GOD'S GUIDANCE FOR US as seen in His guidance of the shepherds in Luke 2:1-20

1. Guidance from God comes to all kinds of people, including the poor and the lowly.
2. It can come to the most surprising kinds of people, even some who are not known for their godliness and spirituality.
3. It comes often to people who are ready to receive it and to do something with it.
4. It can come in very surprising and startling ways.
5. It often comes to people who are in the middle of performing their normal, routine, daily tasks.
6. It always comes at the right time.

7. It can demand that we leave what we are doing at the moment and go somewhere else to do something else.
8. It regularly changes our lives for the better.
9. It often requires and expects immediate belief and obedience. (e.g. the words of the shepherds: "Let us go and see this thing which has happened." Note that they did not say, "IF it has happened.")
10. It must always take precedence over other responsibilities we may have at the time.
11. It can come all at once (or piecemeal and gradually as it did for the Magi).

WORSHIP-Luke 2:1-20

Lessons about WORSHIP from the worship of the angels and the shepherds seen in Luke 2:1-20

1. Worship can be entered into by men or by angels.
2. It can involve loud speaking (or singing). (See Revelation 5:9)
3. It can involve "glorifying and praising God" because of what one has experienced.
4. It can and should excite wonderment, as one tells his or her experience to others who have not had the same experience as he or she.
5. It can be carried out by people of any social class, even the very lowest class in society.
6. It can be accomplished anywhere, even out in an open field.
7. It can take place because we have been overcome by some great thing God has done for us.
8. It should lead to the obedience of God's commandments found in His Word. (See Luke 2:21-24)

WITNESSING FOR THE LORD-Luke 2:20

Lessons about WITNESSING FOR THE LORD from the witnessing of the shepherds after they had met the Christ-child as described in Luke 2:20

1. Witnessing is expected of all those who have experienced the Savior.
2. It can bring other people to the Savior too.

3. It can be ridiculed by unbelievers who think believers are out of their minds.
4. It should grow out of a firsthand, eyewitness experience with the Christ-child.
5. It can be done by all classes of people, even the very humblest and lowest.
6. It is simply telling truthfully what one has seen and heard.
7. It should not be hesitantly and apathetically done.
8. It can have long-range impact.
9. It may not always bear fruit at the time it is done.
10. It does not require a study of theology but just a simple telling of what one has experienced.

TEMPTATIONS-Luke 4:1-14

Lessons about TEMPTATIONS from Satan's tempting of Jesus seen in Luke 4:1-14

1. Temptations will often come when we are physically exhausted.
2. They will often come when we are alone.
3. They will often tempt us to doubt God's Word to us.
4. They can be overcome by a proper use of God's Word. (See Psalm 119:11)
5. They should be resisted immediately, not later.
6. They will come at a point in our lives when it may seem possible to yield without anyone knowing about it.
7. They are not sinful, only yielding to them is.
8. They can be very severe, even life-threatening.
9. They often come when we are "off duty."
10. They must be resisted completely and immediately if we are to overcome them successfully.

A SMALL GROUP-Luke 6:12-15

Lessons regarding A SMALL GROUP from the small group which Jesus chose to be with Him from the larger group of His disciples as seen in Luke 6:12-15 (Compare Mark 3:14 "with Him")

1. A small group can be very good support for an individual in ministry.
2. It can be more manageable and teachable.
3. It can develop more easily a close intimacy and friendship.
4. It can more easily become like its leader.
5. It makes it easier to ask questions, to share burdens, and to pray for personal and common needs.
6. It can be more easily trained for future ministries.

PRAYING-Luke 6:12-19

Lessons regarding PRAYING from Jesus' praying before choosing His twelve disciples in Luke 6:12-19

1. Praying ought to precede any major decision.
2. It can demand solitude.
3. It can require a long period of time. (Here: "a whole night")
4. It is a two-way communication with God.
5. It can include many requests.
6. It may bring answers we never expected or can explain. (Here: Judas Iscariot was an answer to prayer.)
7. It is never a waste of time.
8. It is often a preparation for a ministry that can be tiring even though miraculous. (See Luke 6:17-19)
9. It can prepare the way for a ministry of teaching and of healings.
10. It can make persons useful to others who have serious, even life-threatening problems.
11. It is very important when attempting to deal with demonic, unclean spirits.

OUR LORD'S EXPECTATIONS OF HIS DISCIPLES-Luke 6:17-38

Lessons about OUR LORD'S EXPECTATIONS OF HIS DISCIPLES as expressed in Luke 6:17-38

1. Our Lord's expectations of his disciples can be very difficult to live by in our world.
2. They will make us like our Lord, if we follow them.

3. They are not given in the form of suggestions but commands.
4. They are to be continually practiced, not spasmodically.
5. They can be an aid to making enemies into friends.

DISCIPLES OF JESUS-Luke 6:27-38

Lessons about DISCIPLES OF JESUS from His portrayal of His disciple in Luke 6:27-38

1. Disciples of Jesus will never arrive at perfection or full holiness in this life.
2. They should never quit striving for it in this life.
3. They will be always changing, hopefully for the better, here in this life.
4. They have been given certain specific things to do by their Lord.
5. They may seem odd to the unbelieving world.
6. They need to hear what the Lord commands and obey Him.
7. They can become "doormats" on occasion.
8. They may be taken advantage of on occasion.
9. They may have enemies who dislike them greatly.
10. They are expected to love their enemies and show it by deeds.

BIBLICAL LOVE FOR OTHERS-Luke 6:27-38

Lessons on BIBLICAL LOVE FOR OTHERS from Jesus' teaching about it in Luke 6:27-38

1. Biblical love for others is primarily action, not emotion.
2. It is commanded in God's Word, not something we feel inside us, because feelings cannot be prescribed.
3. It can be expressed, whether one feels like it or not.
4. It should be given without any expectations of its being returned.
5. It is generally commanded in the Bible with various ways in which it can be shown. (e.g. Love your enemies and pray for them; love your enemies and do good to them; if an enemy is hungry, keep on feeding him; etc.)

6. It is proof to those who see it that Christians are truly children of God on high.
7. It is the primary evidence that one is a true disciple of the Lord.
8. It will be evidence that one is truly merciful as His Father in heaven is merciful.
9. It should be extended even to those who are hateful toward Christians.
10. It can be the means of ultimately turning enemies into friends. (implied)

HELPING OTHERS-Luke 6:37-39

Lessons on HELPING OTHERS from the judge, the guide, the teacher, the speck remover, the fruit inspector, and the house builder in Luke 6:37-39

1. Helping others should be done with a proper attitude on the part of the helper.
2. It demands putting one's own life in spiritual order first.
3. It may take the form of leading, teaching, correcting, or fruit-inspecting.
4. It is important business for the kingdom of God.
5. It demands exemplary Christian living on the part of the helper.
6. It must be done with kindness to others and with respect for others.
7. It must be done with purity of motive and with no expectation of a return in kind.
8. It always demands that the helper be teachable also.

TEACHING OTHERS-Luke 6:37-49

Lessons about TEACHING OTHERS from the words of Jesus in Luke 6:37-49

1. Teaching others should come from one who can see spiritual things clearly.
2. It can result in both teacher and students being hurt, if the teacher is "blind."
3. It should be given to a student by word and by example.

4. It has limitations related to the teacher since one cannot lead students farther than he or she has gone in spiritual matters.
5. It can result in a student becoming like his or her teacher, a fact that is scary but true.
6. It provides a Christian teacher with a great opportunity to help his students.
7. It demands careful preparation, earnest prayer, and energetic effort.

PRAYER-Luke 7:1-10

Lessons on PRAYER from the prayer of the centurion for the healing of his servant in Luke 7:1-10

1. Prayer may be repeated for the same thing without it indicating a lack of faith.
2. It must be prayed in faith that the Lord hears and answers prayer.
3. It may be offered by anyone, Jew or Gentile, a person of high social status or low.
4. It can indicate a concern about some special need, a care that is strong enough to be made into a prayer.
5. It may be offered on behalf of the need of someone else.
6. It may be answered simply by a word from the Lord.
7. It can achieve supernatural results in the physical realm.
8. It can achieve results a long distance away from where the prayer is offered.
9. It is asking that we may receive. See James 4:2
10. It demands faith on the part of the pray-er to receive an answer.

Appendix: Compare Matthew 13:58: And Jesus did not do many miracles there [in Nazareth] because of their lack of faith. What a contrast with the centurion of Luke 7:1-10

FAITH-Luke 7:1-10

Lessons on FAITH from the faith of the centurion in Luke 7:1-10

1. Faith is willing and ready to take Jesus at His Word.
2. It does not need to see before it believes.
3. It is more than mere words.
4. It allows the Lord to work miracles and expects that He will do the impossible for us in answer to prayer.
5. It shows itself in humility and a dependence completely on the Lord.
6. It exists in the most surprising people. ["A Roman centurion and friends"]
7. It can achieve results in the physical realm, not only the spiritual.
8. It assumes that the Lord will respond in some way to a sincere petition on the part of a pray-er.
9. It exists in varying degrees within people. (7:9 Note: the "great faith in this man," superior to any faith Jesus had found in Israel.)
10. It changes circumstances, not just the pray-er in relation to his circumstances.
11. It needs to be based on fact, not fiction. (7:3 "after he heard about Jesus")
12. It can be based on rather slender evidence. (He had not met Jesus or even seen or heard Him teach.)
13. It will show itself in many ways.
    How is it seen here?
    a. The centurion's love for the Jews
    b. His concern that Jesus not go to the trouble of coming to his house
    c. His building a synagogue for them
    d. His affectionate interest in his servant
    e. His speech about his authority as a Roman soldier exercising confidence in a Jew
14. It must triumph over prejudices of all kinds (social, national, financial, etc.).
15. It can exist in people for the needs of another person or persons and be effective.

16. It can be present in spite of conscious unworthiness. (Note the centurion's humility. He was certain that the Lord would help him and his servant in spite of his feelings of unworthiness on his part.)
17. It can be valid, be it weak or strong. (Note: all that sought the Lord's help did not have faith like this man's yet Jesus helped many of them. And He will help us too. People in Israel got help, even though their faith was not as great as this centurion's.)

HUMILITY-Luke 7:1-10

Lessons about HUMILITY from the Roman centurion's in Luke 7:1-10

1. Humility is an attitude that allows the Lord to do miracles for us when it is accompanied by faith.
2. It is reflected not only in the things a person says but also the things he or she does.
3. It is a virtue that the Lord honors greatly in an individual.
4. It can be an evidence of faith in the Lord.
5. It pleases the Lord.
6. It is a right feeling of personal unworthiness that indicates a proper attitude for divine help.
7. It can be found in some of the least likely people.
8. It will keep one from boasting about one's generosity and liberality.
9. It is a feeling of one's own great personal unworthiness in comparison with others so much greater.
10. It is an attitude that will prevent a person from calling attention to his or her own personal worthiness, although others may do so.
11. It will not allow one to brag or even feel like bragging about his or her own accomplishments, great and notable as they may be.
12. It is a proper virtue but should not rule out a proper evaluation of one's spiritual gifts given by God for the good of His church. (See Romans 12:3 and also Exodus 3, 4)

OUR LORD-Luke 7:1-10

Lessons to be learned about OUR LORD from His relationship with the centurion in Luke 7:1-10

1. Our Lord is more than able for any need we bring to Him, no matter how hard.
2. He is able to heal at a distance.
3. He wants and likes to help those who will trust Him with their problems.
4. He has not limited His help only to certain people. (Here: a Roman centurion)
5. He is willing to go out of His way to help those with needs. (See 7:6)
6. He is able to take care of physical needs as well as spiritual.
7. He marvels at some things that happen here.
8. He does what He does well.
9. He honors all faith put in Him.
10. He listens to prayers offered to Him.
11. He responds to intercessory prayer made on behalf of other people and their needs.
12. He is willing to listen to reason also. (See 7:9, 10 He did not continue going.)
13. He has power over life, death and sickness.
14. He has time for the one person with a need, even though multitudes may be thronging His path, seeking for His attention. v. 9
15. He can help us with our needs even though He is not visibly present.
16. He is always approachable and concerned about our needs.

DEATH-Luke 7:11-17

Lessons about DEATH from the death of the widow of Nain's son described in Luke 7:11-17

1. Death is not unconquerable by the Lord.
2. It is under His control.
3. It is not a respect of persons or families. (Note: The man who died here was an only son of a widow.)

4. It is not impossible for Jesus to handle, sooner or later.
5. It brings grief to those who are left.

DOUBT-Luke 7:18-23

Lessons about DOUBT from the doubt about the Lord demonstrated by John the Baptist described in Luke 7:18-23

1. Doubt can hit the most surprising people.
2. It can attack the strongest saints on occasion.
3. It can be brought on and aggravated by disappointing circumstances in one's life. (Note: Jesus was not acting as the Messiah John had expected.)
4. It can come because we have forgotten the Word of God and its promises.
5. It can be eased by recounting the things the Lord has done and is doing.
6. It begins in the mind as a person forgets what the Lord has done.
7. It can lead to discouragement which is a violation of Scripture and hence a sin. (See Philippians 4:4)
8. It can demonstrate itself in the asking of questions which should not need to be asked. (See Luke 7:19, 20, see also Luke 1:18)
9. It is a common tool of the Devil to lead a person to become discouraged.

DEMONS-Luke 8:26-39

Lessons about DEMONS from the account of the healing of the Gadarene demoniac in Luke 8:26-39

1. Demons can speak with God ("pray") and get answers.
2. They know and fear Jesus.
3. They can only possess people with God's permission.
4. They can control a person's actions but are themselves under the Lord's control.
5. They can use the vocal cords of the individual whom they possess.
6. They can cause a person to do fearful things.
7. They can be cast out by Jesus.
8. They are powerless to resist Jesus' will.

9. They have nothing in common with Jesus.
10. They know their future in the abyss.
11. They are powerless in the presence of Jesus' power.
12. They are real beings, not to be explained away as figments of someone's imagination.
13. They can and do rob people of everything worthwhile in this life.
14. They can be present in a single life in great number.
15. They believe in the reality of Jesus Christ and Hades.
16. They believe Jesus is the Son of God.
17. They realize Jesus' power over them.
18. They may give the person they possess unusual powers of strength.
19. They are taken seriously by Jesus.
20. They can be cast out from the possessed, leaving the person normal again.
21. They want to occupy bodies, even those of animals.
22. They can physically control an unsaved person whom they indwell.
23. They have names.
24. They can cause uncivilized and even self-destructive behavior in the person they possess.
25. They should be respected as beings of great power but at the same time not feared because their power is limited by God.

PEOPLE-Luke 8:40-56

Lessons about PEOPLE from the accounts of the healing of Jairus' daughter and the bleeding woman described in Luke 8:40-56

1. People vary in all kinds of ways.
2. They have differing needs and problems which need solutions.
3. They do not all have needs that are obvious to the public eye.
4. They often are severe and internal.
5. They can often hinder the Lord in His work.
6. They often need and even want the Lord's help.
7. They can make it hard for people to get to Jesus for help. (See Luke 8:45)

8. They can come to Jesus with personal needs or for intercession for the needs of others.
9. They never bother Jesus when they come with needs requiring His help. (See Luke 8:49, 50)

THE LORD'S HELP-Luke 8:40-56

Lessons on THE LORD'S HELP which He gave to Jairus' daughter and the bleeding woman as described in Luke 8:40-56

1. The Lord's help often demands that we forget ourselves and present our need humbly to Him.
2. It is generally available simply for the asking.
3. It is available for physical needs as well as spiritual needs.
4. It is offered to those who believe Him and His Word.
5. It generally demands coming to Him in prayer for help.
6. It is given without respect for a person's nationality, social status, age, or physical condition.
7. It is available for the believer especially in life-and-death situations.
8. It can do what the best of human help cannot.
9. It can turn times of distress and desperation into times of joy and thankfulness for those aided.
10. It does not always aid all who touch Jesus but only those who "touch" Him in faith. (See Luke 8:45, 46)
11. It is always done in a complete manner.

PRAYER-Luke 8:40-56

Lessons about PRAYER from the situations of Jairus' daughter and the bleeding woman seen in Luke 8:40-56

1. Prayer does not have to be voiced to be heard. (the woman)
2. It alone shows some faith in the Lord.
3. It can be brought on behalf of another. (Jairus for his daughter.)
4. It can be answered in different ways.
5. It can be answered immediately or after some delay, when the problem has gotten worse.

78

6. It can be ridiculed as a resource for help by some people. (See Luke 8:53)
7. It can be offered for personal needs or family needs.
8. It can always be offered for any need no matter how severe.

DEATH-Luke 8:40-56

Lessons about DEATH from the accounts of the healing of Jairus' daughter and the bleeding woman described in Luke 8:40-56

1. Death can take people of all ages.
2. It is no respecter of persons, social strata, nationalities or official positions in a community.
3. It is no problem for the Lord.
4. It can cause great grief, especially to unbelievers.
5. It is often brought on by severe physical illness.

PHYSICAL ILLNESS-Luke 8:40-56

Lessons about PHYSICAL ILLNESS from the illnesses of the twelve year old girl and the woman who had been hemorrhaging for twelve years in Luke 8:40-56

1. Physical illness can be serious enough to result in death.
2. It can vary in severity.
3. It can be so severe that the medical profession may not know how to cure it.
4. It can be handled by the Lord if it is His will to do so.
5. It may require a miracle to correct the situation.
6. It can affect people of all ages, children and adults.
7. It is never too much for our Lord to handle for those who put their trust in Him.
8. It can be handled by simply "touching" Jesus by faith in His healing power.
9. It can be humanly hopeless and get healed immediately by our Lord.
10. It should never be considered too serious but what it can be brought to the Lord in prayer for His involvement.

TROUBLES IN LIFE-Luke 8:40-56

Lesson regarding TROUBLES IN LIFE from the bleeding of the woman and the death of the daughter in Luke 8:40-56

1. Troubles in life can be very severe in nature.
2. They can cause problems that affect a person personally or that affect us via the suffering of another person close to us.
3. They are never too much for the Lord to handle, no matter how severe.
4. They should be handled with prayer.
5. They demand faith in our Lord's word. (Note His words about the little dead girl: "She is sleeping." v. 52)
6. They can be so severe that unbelievers laugh at the thought of their being corrected. "They began laughing at Jesus." v. 53
7. They can be solved as we "touch" the Lord by a prayer of faith.
8. They can be long-lasting in nature. "twelve years" v. 43
9. They can be beyond the range of human help and deliverance.
10. They can become more intense and severe the longer they are left untreated, even resulting in death.

JESUS, OUR LORD-Luke 8:40-56

Lessons about JESUS, OUR LORD from the accounts of His help granted the bleeding woman and the household of Jairus in Luke 8:40-56

1. Jesus, our Lord, loves to help those in need of His help.
2. He is master of every circumstance in life.
3. He can often be laughed at by worldlings and unbelievers, even at times his own disciples. See v. 45.
4. He can do things that amaze unbelievers.
5. He loves to work with and for individuals.
6. He is often hindered in His works by crowds of people. (Here they were a problem for the woman to get to Jesus.)
7. He looks at events in life differently then people do. (Note: The girl died but to Jesus she was sleeping. See

vv. 52, 53. The crowd was pressing upon Jesus on all sides but one woman alone REALLY touched Him. See vv. 45, 46)

8. He is always approachable with any problem. ("If a care is too small to be made into a prayer, it is too small to be made into a burden.")
9. He should be approached as a first resort rather than a last one in any time of need.
10. He is never bothered by our bringing our needs to Him, no matter how large or small they are. (Here were two big ones.)

OUR LORD'S WORK-Luke 9:10-17

Lessons about OUR LORD'S WORK from His feeding of "the 5,000" recorded in Luke 9:10-17

1. Our Lord's work often depends on the obedience of His followers.
2. It can include the miraculous when necessary.
3. It demands our cooperation with Him quite often.
4. It can involve both physical and spiritual results.
5. It often calls for the use of natural possessions. ("five loaves and two fish")

OUR LORD-Luke 9:10-17

Lessons about OUR LORD from His feeding of "the 5000" recorded in Luke 9:10-17

1. Our Lord can take a little and make it go a long way.
2. He is not wasteful in His working.
3. He appreciates orderliness, carefulness, thrift, and economy even in the small things.
4. He appreciates neatness. (no littering)
5. He is concerned even about the physical needs of His followers.
6. He is able to do the miraculous when such is necessary.
7. He does things in an orderly, efficient manner.
8. He often does not do immediately what can be done by natural means. (He does not lavish wastefully His

miraculous power. The disciples seated the crowd, passed out the food and picked up the leftovers. (John 6:12, 13)

9. He welcomes opportunities to speak to crowds about the kingdom of God. (Luke 9:11)
10. He will use what we give Him, no matter how insignificant it may seem in the light of the need.

THE LORD'S HELP-Luke 9:10-17

Lessons about THE LORD'S HELP from His feeding of the multitude recorded in Luke 9:10-17

1. The Lord's help often comes by help from the Lord's followers.
2. It is always timely but often does come not a lot ahead of time.
3. It is available for all, but especially for the Lord's own.
4. It often exceeds the particular need at the time.
5. It is always exactly what is needed and can be even more than is needed.
6. It is available always for His followers.
7. It often comes in seemingly impossible human situations.
8. It can even come when we have not prayed for it.
9. It should be expected, especially by the Lord's own.
10. It can be an encouragement to us in other bad situations as we remember His help in previous times.
11. It can relate to physical needs, as well as to spiritual and emotional.
12. It often demands the cooperation of His followers.
13. It can come for believers and even for those who are non-believers at the time.
14. It can involve the Lord's working of miracles to fulfill certain needs.
15. It is always in the nick of time.
16. It often comes with the use of His followers.
17. It can be expected, especially in emergency situations.
18. It may be given by the use of natural means.
19. It is generally very generous, more than enough.
20. It may come even before we ask for it. (Note: The crowd did not ask for this.)
21. It often comes in an orderly and calm fashion.

INVOLVEMENT WITH THE NEEDS OF OTHERS-
Luke 10:25-37

Lessons about INVOLVEMENT WITH THE NEEDS OF OTHERS from the involvement of the good Samaritan in the needs of the man beaten and robbed described in Luke 10:25-37

1. Involvement with the needs of others will often take time, effort and expense.
2. It can demand sacrificial giving of money and time.
3. It will often be demanded of us on the spur of the moment.
4. It can involve a radical change of plans which we may have made ahead of time.
5. It will regularly demand action, not just emotion.
6. It will often come as an interruption in our schedules.
7. It will force us to think about what Jesus would do.
8. It will necessarily demand sacrifice from us.
9. It is expected of those who follow the Lord and should be religious.
10. It should be done as completely as humanly possible.
11. It demands a decision.
12. It often demands putting others and their needs ahead of our own.
13. It often demands using what we have in serving others.
14. It is required of real Christians.
15. It can involve personal risk and danger for oneself.
16. It will involve more than just feelings of pity but actions of mercy.
17. It will not let racial, societal, emotional or physical matters prevent one from giving aid. (Note: The one in need of help here was identified as "a certain man" even though he was probably a Jew helped by a Samaritan.)
18. It often demands immediate action without taking a lot of time to think about personal danger or what things should be done.
19. It often demands that a person act alone without anyone else to help.

PEOPLE WHO ARE NEIGHBORS TO PEOPLE AROUND THEM IN NEED-Luke 10:25-37

Lessons about PEOPLE WHO ARE NEIGHBORS TO PEOPLE *AROUND THEM IN NEED from the good Samarian who helped the man who fell among thieves described in Luke 10:25-37*

1. People who are neighbors to others in need around them are prepared to take personal risks for themselves. (The thieves could still have been around.)
2. They have the discipline and self-control to go out of their way, if necessary, to help someone else.
3. They are willing to use their own resources for the good of another.
4. They are willing to take time to minister to others.
5. They are courageous and willing even to act alone, when necessary, to help the needy.
6. They are willing even to give extra time to return and check on the one they have helped and complete their self-chosen responsibility.
7. They are willing cheerfully to practice "the golden rule" of Matthew 7:12.
8. They are willing to minister to anyone in need, no matter what his or her nationality or social position may be. "a man"
9. They often see numerous ways in which they can become involved to help others.
10. They are willing to use whatever they have to be of service. (e.g. physical strength, oil, wine, money, time, etc.)
11. They have a desire to complete the job.
12. They have an active love for others, even total strangers.
13. They are willing even to "put themselves out" and to lose sleep to help another when necessary. (See Luke 10:34)
14. They are willing even to change personal plans to be of service. ("The Samaritan was on a journey.")
15. They will go cheerfully "the extra mile" to help another.
16. They place a higher value on people rather than on personal plans or personal possessions.

17. They ignore the bad examples so often set by others around them. (e.g. the priest and the Levite)
18. They will care for the immediate needs of others and often will consider their ongoing needs as well.
19. They are not so concerned and busy about their own plans and needs that they overlook the needs of others.
20. They are willing to put all they have at the disposal of a person in need of help.

OPPORTUNITIES TO HELP OTHERS GROW-
Luke 10:30-37

Lessons on OPPORTUNITIES TO HELP OTHERS GROWING out of the opportunity given the good Samaritan to help a needy individual in the story told by Jesus in Luke 10:30-37

1. Opportunities to help others often can come at the most unexpected times.
2. They can demand immediate action for any number of reasons.
3. They may be entered into without the one helped even knowing who helped him.
4. They may often be taken advantage of without any thought of reward or payment for the help given.
5. They will often come at the most inopportune moments, interfering with previous plans.
6. They are opportunities for ministry given by our sovereign Lord that must not be missed.
7. They can take a variety of forms and demand a variety of sacrifices.
8. They can involve the helper in great danger to himself or herself, if he or she is not careful.
9. They may involve someone in ministering alone to the one in need.

INDIFFERENCE TO THE NEEDS OF OTHERS-
Luke 10:30-37

Lessons on INDIFFERENCE TO THE NEEDS OF OTHERS growing out of the indifference of the priest and the Levite in the story Jesus told in Luke 10:30-37

1. Indifference to the needs of others can be seen in people who, because of who they are, ought to be very interested in other people and their needs.
2. It can be seen in the most surprising people.
3. It indicates a selfish consideration of oneself rather than thoughtfulness of others and their needs.
4. It is the exact opposite of the attitudes of a sincere follower of the Lord.

MATERIAL POSSESSIONS-Luke 12:13-21

Lessons about MATERIAL POSSESSIONS from the rich fool in the parable that Jesus told in Luke 12:13-21

1. Material possessions are not sinful but can be very dangerous.
2. They can lead a person to a point in life when he or she forgets the God who allowed him to gain such wealth.
3. They cannot satisfy the deepest needs of a person's life.
4. They cannot support or satisfy a person's soul.
5. They cannot be taken with us when we leave this life.
6. They can be treasured up for oneself but cannot necessarily make a person rich toward God.
7. They can become barriers to trusting God, our Savior, for our lives here and now and in the future.
8. They are given to use to aid others, not to be lavished on ourselves.
9. They can fool us into thinking we are independent and in need of no one or nothing else.
10. They are some of the good things that God gives to us to lead us to repentance. (See Romans 2:4)

WORRYING-Luke 12:22-34

Lessons about WORRYING from the teaching of Jesus about worry in Luke 12:22-34

1. Worrying comes naturally to us as human beings.
2. It is a violation of Scripture and hence a sin to be avoided. (See Philippians 4:6, 7)
3. It is an illegitimate concern about the future.

4. It tends to dominate and consume our minds and thought life.
5. It is characteristic of a life that lacks a trust in a heavenly Father and has forgotten His promises to His children.
6. It robs the worrier of the inner peace which God wants all His children to enjoy. (See Philippians 4:4-7, especially v. 7)
7. It is futile and regularly counterproductive. (As someone has said, "It is like a rocking chair. It gives one something to do but won't get the person doing it anywhere.")
8. It sets a bad example for those around us.
9. It is a painful experience from which God wants to spare us and can spare us if we put our trust wholly in Him and His Word.
10. It is a characteristic of people who have their "treasure" laid up down here where it can disappear so rapidly and so easily.

PEOPLE-Luke 16:19-31

Lessons about PEOPLE from Jesus' description of the rich man and Lazarus in Luke 16:19-31

1. People exist in this life in all sorts of conditions, such as in wealth, in poverty, in pain, and without consideration for others in severe need of help.
2. They can be very selfish with the things they have, especially those who have a lot of this world's goods.
3. They may not be concerned about their own spiritual needs or the needs of others until they get a taste of the next life.
4. They often find it hard to believe the warnings of Scripture about the life after death until it has become too late to believe and be saved.
5. They often pray instinctively when they get into tough and painful circumstances.
6. They will be separated permanently into one of two groups once they die physically.

7. They will be totally conscious in a place of pain or pleasure once they die physically. (For the believers who die today, see II Corinthians 5:6-8 and Philippians 1:21-23.)
8. They will go on living somewhere as completely spiritual beings after they die physically, the body having been buried to await whichever resurrection they will have a part in. (See John 5:28, 29)
9. They can be so intelligent and money-wise relative to material things and so foolish and unwise relative to spiritual and heavenly matters.
10. They can be with many other people in the same locality (here: Hades) and yet feel so alone. (See Luke 16:26 where the Greek word "you" is used twice in the plural, indicating that others were with the rich man in Hades.)

PHYSICAL DEATH-Luke 16:19-31

Lessons about PHYSICAL DEATH from the deaths of the rich man and Lazarus described in Luke 16:19-31 (Note: This does not seem to be a parable because people are not named in parables, e.g. Lazarus and Abraham.)

1. Physical death does not end one's existence or one's consciousness.
2. It finalizes one's spiritual condition for all eternity. (See Hebrews 9:27)
3. It can result in our going to a place of good things and happiness or a place of unrest and evil things.
4. It is a condition in which the soul is disembodied for a time. (See II Corinthians 5:14: The soul exists in "a kind of naked state." It is described physically for our better understanding. Abraham did not have a bosom nor did Lazarus have a finger nor did the rich man have a tongue at this time of their lives. These bodily parts were all buried with their bodies.)
5. It can be a joyfully anticipated event or a very fearful one.
6. It can lead to immediate joy or immediate misery and great torment.

7. It can be prepared for by a careful study and heeding of the Scriptures. (See Luke 16:31)
8. It can result in a reversal of circumstances when compared with the conditions a person has known in this life. (See Luke 16:25)
9. It often is experienced by one member of a family at a time and should be a warning to other members of one's family, who are left, to prepare for their own deaths. (See Luke 16:27, 28)
10. It is a serious event in a person's life but not one to be feared if one has taken care of eternal matters in this life before death comes.

LIFE AFTER PHYSICAL DEATH-Luke 16:19-31

Lessons about LIFE AFTER PHYSICAL DEATH from the deaths of the rich man and Lazarus told by Jesus in Luke 16:19-31

1. Life after physical death is characterized by complete consciousness.
2. It is determined by people before they die based on how they have responded to God's Word. (See Luke 16:31)
3. It cannot be changed once we have died.
4. It is a sure thing according to the Bible.
5. It will be immediately bodiless, blessed, enjoyable and restful if one has accepted Jesus by faith.
6. It will be immediately bodiless but very painful for those who have not accepted Jesus by faith.
7. It does exist.
8. It is something for which a person needs to prepare in this life here on earth.
9. It is eternally important.
10. It is not determined by whether a person is rich or poor in this life. (This is not clear from Jesus' account here but is clear from a comparison of other Scriptures which speak of repentance and faith as necessary for salvation and eternal life. See Luke 16:30; Acts 3:19; 17:30; 26:20; John 1:12; 3:16; and Romans 3:21-31) Appendix: Note that this account is not said to be a parable. People are not usually named in parables. In this story Abraham and Lazarus are named.

OUR LORD'S SECOND COMING-Luke 21:5-36

Lessons about OUR LORD'S SECOND COMING from Luke 21:5-36

1. Our Lord's second coming will not be a quiet affair.
2. It will be preceded by many signs.
3. It will require preparation by the saints alive at the time.
4. It will follow a great tribulation; a time of great suffering for believers.
5. It will take place on an unknown day and at an unknown hour.
6. It will be over quickly once it has begun.
7. It will leave no time for repentance and other preparations.
8. It will be a time of redemption and glory for the saints.
9. It will be preceded by severe convulsions in the heavens.
10. It will be a cause for great fear on the part of many on earth.
11. It will be visible for people on the earth.
12. It will affect all mankind in some way.
13. It will be a time of deliverance for all Christians.
14. It will come after destruction of the Jewish temple.
15. It will come unexpectedly for those who are not ready for it.

Acts

A SPIRITUALLY HEALTHY CHURCH-Acts 5:12-16

Lessons about A SPIRITUALLY HEALTHY CHURCH to be gained from the spiritually healthy church described in Acts 5:12-16.

1. A spiritually healthy church is one with spiritual vision, seeing God's power at work in all areas of life.
2. It is filled with believers who lovingly act as brothers and sisters in Christ, working for the good of the whole body.
3. It is one whose members give of themselves and their means wholeheartedly, holding themselves accountable to God and each other.
4. It is humble in its walk with Christ, pointing others to him.
5. It rejoices when the Spirit draws new believers to Himself and welcomes them into the fellowship of believers.
6. It is one whose members truly follow Christ's example, living lives characterized by righteousness, faithfulness, and self-sacrifice, so that nothing hinders others from seeing Christ in them.
7. It attracts the attention of outsiders.
8. It is held in high esteem by people outside its fellowship. (See Acts 5:13)
9. It is a group to which people can go for healing and help of all kinds.
10. It is a body of believers who expect to see and are seeing miracles happening in their midst.
11. It is not afraid to meet together in public places to let its "light" shine. (See Acts 5:12 "Solomon's portico")
12. It has members who enjoy being together on a regular basis.
13. It is one that grows in number because people are being helped on a regular and miraculous basis.
14. It is one that has respect for its leadership. ("The apostles"–Acts 5:12 and "Peter"–Acts 5:15)
15. It is one that encourages people who have needs to come together to find help, even miraculous help. (See Acts 5:16)

ENEMIES OF THE GOSPEL-Acts 5:17-33

Lesson about ENEMIES OF THE GOSPEL MESSAGE from the enemies described in Acts 5:17-33

1. Enemies of the gospel message can be people who are religious.
2. They often refuse to recognize and embrace what is obviously true.
3. They often attempt to justify their opposition to the gospel.
4. They will attempt to stop the spread of the truth of the gospel by various means.
5. They cannot nor will they ultimately succeed in their attacks on the gospel message or messengers.
6. They often are enraged because they cannot succeed in their attacks.
7. They do not want to hear the gospel because it is convicting to their hearts.
8. They behave in ways consistent with their unregenerate natures.
9. They are often very zealous in their efforts to suppress the truth and maintain the status quo.
10. They do not like being held responsible for their sinful, hateful actions.
11. They often become jealous as the believers grow in number and influence.
12. They do not want other groups to have more influence than they do.
13. They often become puzzled and confused when God supports His own people with miracles that cannot be doubted or explained.
14. They often live in fear of what others may say or do to them.
15. They often think that the gospel will die out if they can silence the bold testimonies of its witnesses.

HINDRANCES TO GOD'S PROGRAM-Acts 6, 7

Lessons on HINDRANCES TO GOD'S PROGRAM as seen in the seeming hindrances to God's program in Acts 6, 7

1. Hindrances to God's program can be used to advance this program rather than to hinder it. (The stoning of Stephen resulted in the salvation of Saul of Tarsus.)
2. They often begin when God is obviously blessing His people and Satan wants to stop that.
3. They are really only seeming "set-backs" because they can be opportunities for church growth and rejoicing.
4. They often result from jealousy over the success the church is having.
5. They should be recognized as only temporary because God is still at work through them and will triumph ultimately and eternally.
6. They do not deter a Spirit-filled and faith-full person from continuing to obey Christ in proclaiming the Gospel and making disciples for Him.
7. They are to be expected when and where God is working.
8. They can often be violent, murderous and horrific, but always ultimately unsuccessful.
9. They can always be overcome with God's help and His instructions found in the Bible.
10. They will often increase in intensity the more we let God use us.
11. They can take the form of persecuting people whom God is using in spectacular ways.
12. They do not have to be roadblocks to God's successful working if they are handled carefully and in keeping with God's instructions in His Word. (e.g. the handling of the neglect of the Greek widows)
13. They can involve internal problems within the church or external problems outside the church.
14. They are never nice to experience but can be some of the "all things that God can continue working out together for good" for His church. (See Romans 8:28)
15. They will never be more than we can handle with God's gracious help. (See I Corinthians 10:13)

HANDLING CHURCH CRISES-Acts 6:1-7

Lessons about HANDLING CHURCH CRISES from the church crisis which was handled by the church members in Acts 6:1-7

1. We should diligently try to avoid church crises in the first place.
2. We should seek out carefully trusted, Spirit-filled people to solve the crisis.
3. We should select qualified people to give their attention to the correction of the problems.
4. We should do all we can to make sure that the church's ministry staff is not overloaded so they can give priority attention to their main duties.
5. We should handle church crises in ways that reflect the fruit of the Spirit in our lives.
6. We should discuss problems with carefulness, making sure that all involved are heard and treated fairly.
7. We should choose lay-leaders who are Spirit-led, not those who are popular, financially well off or related to other members of the congregation.
8. We should expect that our ministers are able to give themselves to the ministry of the Word and prayer so they can lead their congregation in a godly and scripturally intelligent way.
9. We should be willing to share responsibility within the church family, encouraging and allowing all to use their specific gifts for the glory of God and the good of the church.
10. We should not neglect voicing legitimate concerns but it should be done in a loving and a peaceable way.
11. We should be willing to put others' interests ahead of our own.
12. We should trust chosen leaders who are Spirit-filled to handle crises fairly and squarely.
13. We should work at solving any crisis immediately, justly, directly, and lovingly.
14. We should give careful attention to rumblings of discontent and take action immediately.

15. We should ascertain the abilities of people in the local congregation and then determine how best to use them.

WAYS IN WHICH TROUBLES OF VARIOUS KINDS IN THE CONTEMPORARY CHURCH CAN BE TAKEN CARE OF-Acts 6:1-15

Lessons regarding WAYS IN WHICH TROUBLES OF VARIOUS KINDS IN THE CONTEMPARARY CHURCH CAN BE TAKEN CARE OF from the fixing of the problems by the early church reflected in Acts 6:1-15

1. Troubles in the church today should be faced head-on.
2. They should be taken immediately and directly to their church leadership for resolution.
3. They should be handled by Spirit-filled and Spirit-directed people.
4. They may demand the delegation of specific responsibilities to different people according to the practices and gifts given variously by the Holy Spirit. (Contrast here the apostles and the laity.)
5. They should not be allowed to fester and thus risk infecting the whole body of believers.
6. They may start with the murmuring of certain people in the congregation who feel they or their family members are being overlooked in the daily administrates of the church program.
7. They can split a congregation in two if they are allowed to continue.
8. They should be handled in loving and positive ways.
9. They should not be treated as though they did not exist.
10. They may be best handled by those immediately affected by them. (Note the appointment of seven Greeks to handle the situation, that is, if the names of the seven "deacons" here are any indication. – They were apparently all Greeks.)
11. They can result in greater growth and miraculous conversions when they are handled peacefully and lovingly by the church leadership. (See Acts 6:7)

96

TRIBULATIONS OF GOD'S PEOPLE-Acts 6:8-15

Lessons about TRIBULATIONS FOR GOD'S PEOPLE from the tribulations suffered by the church members in Acts 6:8-15 and 7:51-60

1. Tribulations for God's people often come to those who are closely following God's leading.
2. They may take the form of slanderous words, mistreatment in other ways, physical abuse, imprisonment, or even painful death.
3. They can and should provide opportunities to exhibit God's sustaining grace to those seeing the Christians suffer as true Christians.
4. They can provide times for powerful Christian teaching to those who do not believe. (Note Stephen's sermon to the Sanhedrin)
5. They do not necessarily mean that God is not with His suffering people or is ignorant of their sufferings.
6. They should cause one to rely on God's aid and the support of His promises rather than on their own strength.
7. They can be overcome by the power of the Holy Spirit. (See Acts 7:34)

Philippians

REJOICING-Philippians 1-4

Lessons about REJOICING from Philippians 1-4, a key thought throughout the entire book

1. Rejoicing is an action which can be done in good and bad circumstances.
2. It is not primarily an emotion or a feeling.
3. It can help anyone in times of suffering.
4. It can set an example for others when they are going through tough times.
5. It can be difficult to practice many times.
6. It is something expected of all believers at all times good or bad.
7. It does not always come automatically.
8. It can be done, regardless of one's feelings in certain grievous circumstances.
9. It can be commanded because it is an action.
10. It can be practiced because of a knowledge of one's Lord, His promises and His nearness.
11. It reflects a strong faith in the nearness of the Lord (Philippians 4:5) and one's trust in His promises (Philippians 4:7).
12. It can be done anywhere at any time in any circumstances.
13. It is rarely easy to do in adverse circumstances but is always a Christian's option.
14. It can be practiced in spite of our not knowing "why" adverse things are happening to us.
15. It can help us avoid worrying about any problem in life, as can also repeated praying about any matter. (See Philippians 4:6)
16. It can result in further rejoicing when any difficulty we are experiencing at some time is passed through successfully with the Lord's help.
17. It shows we are focused on our position in the Lord and not on our circumstances, as difficult as they may be.
18. It does not mean that we are always happy.
19. It is an evidence of our contentment in every situation. (See Philippians 4:11-12)

It should be a hallmark trait of Christians which separates the believer from the children of this age.

Colossians

CHRISTIAN LIVING-Colossians 3 and 4

Lessons about CHRISTIAN LIVING from Colossians 3 and 4

1. Christian living should be characterized by thankfulness from all believers.
2. It should look very different from worldly living.
3. It is different because it is being lived by people whose minds are set on and guided by things above.
4. It begins with the putting on of the new self.
5. It should be characterized by incessant prayerfulness.
6. It can bring expected hardships and tests of all kinds.
7. It has an eternal perspective in view at all times.
8. It is characterized by death to all kinds of sinning.

THE CHRISTIAN FAMILY-Colossians 3 and 4

Lessons on THE CHRISTIAN FAMILY from the references to the family in Colossians 3 and 4

1. The Christian family should follow the orders given here.
2. It should be united in love, exemplified by the husband and father.
3. It should be led by one husband (male) and one wife (female).
4. It should be biblically guided.
5. It exists to do all it does for the glory of God.
6. It should be known for its praying together.
7. It should work and serve together as a unit.
8. It should be saturated with thankfulness to God for His blessings.
9. It should not spoil its relationship with favoritism of any kind.
10. It has discipline within its ranks as one of its responsibilities.
11. It is headed by spouses who respect and love each other.
12. It is headed by the husband and father.

13. It is characterized by gracious conversation among the family members.
14. It sets a good example to be copied by those outside the immediate family circle, even by those who are not believers.
15. It should be characterized by husbands loving their wives, wives subjecting themselves to their husbands, and children obeying their parents.
16. It is a teamwork proposition to be successful.
17. It takes will-power and effort so that it can be a "heaven" on earth.
18. It should be characterized by family members who make an effort not to antagonize one another.
19. It is expected of Christian people.
20. It is to be patriarchally ordered.

Thessalonians

CONCERN FOR OTHERS-I Thessalonians 1-3

Lessons about CONCERN FOR OTHERS from Paul's concern seen in I Thessalonians 1-3

1. Concern for others can and should be shown in both speech and action.
2. It is evidenced by a person's willingness to suffer persecution for others and even to risk one's life itself.
3. It is evidenced in an inquiry after the health of the faith of others.
4. It will be proved by one person's attempts to stay in touch with others.
5. It is a mark of true Christian friendship.
6. It is a characteristic of a growing, maturing Christian and of effective Christian leadership.
7. It should be manifested especially toward people who are going through hard times.
8. It is a foundation for good personal relations with others.
9. It can take the form of one inquiring after another's spiritual well-being.
10. It should be honestly and sincerely shown in as many ways as possible.
11. It can take the form of assisting others financially. (See I Thessalonians 2:9)
12. It should be dispensed with the gentleness of a nursing mother (I Thessalonians 2:7) or a loving father (I Thessalonians 2:11).
13. It should be exemplary for all around who see it.
14. It can lead to incessant prayer for others and their needs. (I Thessalonians 1:2)
15. It should be a priority in our lives over concern for ourselves.
16. It can be shown at a high personal cost of time and effort.
17. It can involve one's personal suffering for others in need.
18. It requires living a holy life in order to set an example for others.

19. It does not necessarily mean that you have to be with them in person. (There are long-range ways of showing one's love. I Thessalonians 3:2)
20. It can be thwarted by Satan in various ways. (See I Thessalonians 1:18)

SUFFERING FOR CHRIST-I Thessalonians 1-3
Lessons about SUFFERING FOR CHRIST from the discussion of suffering in I Thessalonians 1-3

1. Suffering for Christ can be brought on by one's reception of salvation offered in God's Word, the Gospel. (I Thessalonians 1:6)
2. It hopefully makes us good examples for other believers to copy. (I Thessalonians 1:7)
3. It can make our faith shine forth brightly for miles around. (I Thessalonians 1:8)
4. It should not cause us to give up our ministry, even if we have been mistreated in a few places. (I Thessalonians 2:2)
5. It should be undergone with a boldness in our God to continue to speak forth the gospel of God clearly. (I Thessalonians 2:2)
6. It should never lead us to soft-pedal the gospel in order to please men or to get the glory of men or to avoid suffering. (I Thessalonians 2:4)
7. It will come because often unsaved people do not like to hear or to receive the gospel. (I Thessalonians 2:2)
8. It should never make us hard and bitter but gentle and tender as a nursing [mother] cares for her children. (I Thessalonians 2:7)
9. It is not unique or peculiar to one class of people or to one location; but many different classes of people have experienced suffering for Christ in many different places. (I Thessalonians 2:14)
10. It can take the form of hindering the giving of the gospel to certain groups of people who are in great need of salvation. (I Thessalonians 2:16)
11. It can take the form of Satanic attacks or hindrances to the spreading of the Gospel. (I Thessalonians 2:18)

12. It can be and should be accepted with joy in the hope of the Lord's return to bring suffering for his saints to an end. (I Thessalonians 2:19-20)
13. It can be faced much more easily when a stronger Christian comes alongside us to strengthen and to encourage us in our faith. (I Thessalonians 3:2)
14. It should not trouble or disturb us because the Scriptures tell us that we are destined for suffering. (I Thessalonians 3:3)
15. It is to be expected by all faithful believers according to God's prophetic Word. (I Thessalonians 3:4)
16. It need not overcome us any more than it did the Thessalonians. (I Thessalonians 3:6)
17. It demands that we stand FIRM in the Lord, no matter how severe the testing may be. (I Thessalonians 3:8)

Timothy

FAITH-I Timothy 1

Lessons on FAITH from I Timothy 1

1. Faith will show itself in action.
2. It must be given its proper place in our lives.
3. It demands information and instruction.
4. It can be lost if one is not careful.
5. It will be seen clearly by the things which a person avoids like a plague, the vices listed here.
6. It will give proper place to God's law in our lives.
7. It involves complete trust in God in any circumstance of life.
8. It will involve doing, even when fighting the good fight. (See I Timothy 1:18)
9. It is an important attribute of every Christian's life and must be retained at all costs.
10. It is not only a term for "trust" but for "the Christian way of life," not only for faith but for the faith.

CHRISTIAN LOVE-I Timothy 1:5-14

Lessons on CHRISTIAN LOVE from I Timothy 1:5-14

1. Christian love will grow out of a pure heart, a clear conscience, and a sincere faith.
2. It should be expressed to others more often.
3. It should be expressed not only by word but by actions as well.
4. It should be the goal of our living.
5. It can be lost so easily in "fighting the good fight." (See I Timothy 1:18)
6. It should be characterized by sincerity, no hypocrisy or sham or pretense.
7. It is active and volitional, not basically emotional.
8. It is missing so many places.
9. It is the distinguishing mark of a Christian person.
10. It should be the object of our preaching and teaching.

The proof of our learning is in our living. Teaching is not all a matter of mind but a manner of life. Our Christianity should affect our attitudes and our actions.

Hebrews

ANGELS-Hebrews 1

Lesson about ANGELS from the teaching of Hebrews 1

1. Angels do not hold a higher position than Jesus, God's Son.
2. They are ministering spirits sent forth to serve the saved, the heirs of salvation.
3. They are worshippers, not objects to be worshiped.
4. They are commanded to worship the Son and to be subject to Him.
5. They are changeable as wind and fire, not eternal as the Son.
6. They are in submission to God.
7. They have names that are less significant than God's Son's name.
8. They do exist although many people have never seen one.

GOD SPEAKING TO US-Hebrews 1

Lessons about GOD SPEAKING TO US from the teaching of Hebrews 1

1. God's speaking to us comes to us today through the entire Bible.
2. It was not always complete in the past.
3. It is clearer now than in Old Testament times.
4. It became much clearer and more complete with the coming of Christ, the Son.
5. It is often ignored and neglected.
6. It can include the use of texts from various parts of the Old Testament.
7. It has become much clearer with God speaking to us by His Son. (John 14:9)
8. It can take different forms, even as it did in the Old Testament.
9. It should always be given serious attention.
10. It cannot force us to listen.

SPIRITUAL DRIFTING-Hebrews 2

Lessons about SPIRITUAL DRIFTING from Hebrews 2

1. Spiritual drifting results in a believer going farther away from God.
2. It happens when a person refuses to hear and obey God's Word.
3. It often happens by choice, not chance.
4. It is very dangerous.
5. It can be avoided by persistent attention to what we have been taught from God's Word.
6. It can be very gradual, almost unnoticeable.
7. It leads to spiritual dullness and insensitivity to spiritual matters.
8. It can result ultimately in a forfeiture of salvation.
9. It can cause others to drift and even leave the faith since it is often contagious.
10. It is manifested in a lack of caring about spiritual matters.
11. It stunts and even stops spiritual growth.
12. It is often easier when one keeps company with the wrong kind of friends.
13. It can happen because of carelessness.
14. It will not necessarily make the Lord give up on the drifter.
15. It can happen to anyone.

NOBODY EVER DRIFTED INTO SPIRITUAL
EXCELLENCE.

TESTING GOD-Hebrews 3

Lessons about TESTING GOD from Hebrews 3

1. Testing God is forbidden by the Scriptures.
2. It can grow out of selfishness.
3. It can lead to dire consequences.
4. It can grow out of unbelieving and unfaithfulness.
5. It can result in a loss of spiritual rest.
6. It arouses God's anger.
7. It can bring about severe spiritual conviction.

8. It can keep God's promises from being fulfilled for us or at least delayed.

9. It stems from an evil heart of unbelief.

10. It is sinful.

11. It can result from backsliding.

12. It can result in a hardening of heart.

13. It can make entering God's "rest" less likely, if not impossible.

14. It will not go unpunished.

15. It is contagious.

16. It shows a shortness of memory and a forgetting of God's past blessings.

17. It can be done by a group or an individual.

18. It can hinder our reception of God's blessings.

19. It can result in a "desert" experience in our lives.

20. It shows a lack of reverence for and of a fear of God.

LIVING THE CHRISTIAN LIFE TODAY-Hebrews 3

Lessons on LIVING THE CHRISTIAN LIFE TODAY from Hebrews 3

1. Living the Christian life today demands being on guard against unbelief.
2. It is our heavenly calling.
3. It is a life of confidence and hope.
4. It involves a lifelong commitment.
5. It can be carried out more easily with the encouragement of others.
6. It must be centered around Christ and the example He has set.
7. It demands that we be continually spiritually alert.
8. It requires perseverance through and endurance of trials of all sorts.
9. It demands holding fast to our faith and to the Faith.
10. It demands hearing God's voice and obeying it.
11. It demands a remembrance that testing God is dangerous to be avoided at all costs.

BACKSLIDING-Hebrews 5:11-14

Lessons on BACKSLIDING from Hebrews 5:11-14

1. Backsliding makes it difficult for Christians to understand the truth.
2. It makes them less advanced in Christian truth so that they are unable to be the teachers they should be as a result of the length of time they have been Christians.
3. It can put them in a position where they need the elementary truths of the Christian faith taught to them again.
4. It dulls their senses regarding matters related to good and evil.
5. It demonstrates a severe lack of Christian maturity.
6. It shows a severe lack of self-discipline as Christians.
7. It comes from spiritual apathy and laziness.
8. It makes it hard, if not impossible, for the backslider to assimilate spiritually solid "food."
9. It prevents the backslider from progressing from the "babyhood" stage to the "adult teaching" stage.
10. It prevents one from reaching the stage where he or she can understand and discuss deeper truths related to righteousness.
11. It can be prevented by exercise and training one's senses to tell the difference between good and evil.
12. It happens when one is not moving forward but drifting in the Christian faith.
13. It is something that should be seriously addressed for the church.
14. It is generally not something that just unconsciously happens but is a result of one's choices.
15. It is a very real danger for the unwary Christian.
16. It can involve a person's <u>becoming</u> something he or she once was not.
17. It needs to be avoided at all legitimate costs.
18. It is not what God or our spiritual leaders desire for any Christian.
19. It can have very serious repercussions in the lives of people. (See Hebrews 6:4-6)

20. It can be avoided by the constant, persevering exercise of one's senses for the discernment of both good and evil.

Titus

GOOD WORKS-Titus 2 and 3

Lessons on GOOD WORKS from Titus 2 and 3

Titus   2:7   "We are in all things to show ourselves to be an example of good works..."

      2:13   We have been redeemed from every lawless work and redeemed as people zealous for good works.

      3:1   "We are to be ready for every good work."

      3:5   "We are not saved on the basis of works which we have done in righteousness but according to His mercy..."

      3:8   "We are to be careful to engage in good works that are good and profitable for all mankind (tois anthropois.)"

1. Good works are not the grounds for our salvation but an evidence of it.
2. They indicate a turnaround in a person's thinking.
3. They are intended to glorify God, not the doer.
4. They are clearly God's will for the believer.
5. They are good and profitable for all mankind.
6. They are to be done by all believers.
7. They are an evidence of love for everyone.
8. They are caused by Christians considering the needs of others more important than their own.
9. They often require diligent effort to complete.
10. They are done as an indicator of our subjection to God and to those earthly authorities He has placed over us.
11. They can promote community life that is healthier and happier for all community members.
12. They should come naturally for a believer.
13. They are desired by God from every believer.
14. They make the Christian's life a productive one.
15. They are part of God's plan for His people and their lives.
16. They can demand preparation by the Christian.
17. They do not save us but prove that the faith of the doer is real.

18. They should not be done with a rebellious or unloving spirit.
19. They can meet the pressing needs of other people.
20. They are things that a Christian should do with zeal and great desire.

Index

A

B

C

D

E

114

L

M

116

Dr. Wesley L. Gerig.....

taught for fifty-one years at Fort Wayne Bible College, Summit Christian College, and Taylor University Fort Wayne (one campus-three different names), retiring in 2008. Dr. Wes, as he was known around campus, was Professor of Bible, Theology and Biblical Languages. While teaching just about every book in the Bible, he collected many illustrations and outlines which he has kept and now complied in two volumes, *Lessons From Life For Life*, the first of which is in your hands.

Besides teaching, Dr. Gerig has served many churches as interim pastor, offering biblical teaching and counsel during times of pastoral transition. He has also traveled extensively including the Dominican Republic, Ecuador, Greece, Jamaica, Japan, the Phillipines, Russia and Taiwan and three trips to the Middle East.

Other books by Dr. Gerig

Romans: An Outline Study
Dr. Gerig outlines the book of Romans in a 213-page exegetical work, which uncovers for the reader Paul's Epistle to the Romans methodical and progressive treatment of the doctrine of justification by faith. Along with the outline, His personal translation of the epistle for the non-Greek reader is included also a series of factual and discussion projects based on the text.

What We Believe and Why: Our Faith in Outline Form
This 288-page systematic theology book is essentially the culmination of Dr. Wes Gerig's 51 years of teaching on the Fort Wayne campus. It summarizes the historic belief of the Church, presents other views, and evaluate those other views Biblically.

The Core Of Christian Love
Jesus said, "If you love me, you will keep my commandments." What are these commandments? Dr. Wes Gerig, former Fort Wayne professor tackles these commandments and this topic in The Core of Christian Love: Love as Action. In preparation for this book, he read through the entire New Testament, wrote down every commandment according to his own personal translation from the Greek text, and categorized them.

Lessons from Life for Life-Old Testament
Lessons from Life for Life provides practical life applications based on more than 168 Old Testament passages and 180 topics helping the reader to apply and do what the Word says. This 256-page resource is great for pastors, individuals and small-groups while studying God's Word.

www.ingramcontent.com/pod-product-compliance
Lightning Source LLC
Chambersburg PA
CBHW051043030426
42339CB00006B/175